ONE
A JOURNEY BEGINS

*To: Mrs Powell
May you always be blessed.
Love
Gwen
Thanks*

GWEN COLLINS WOMACK

COPYRIGHT © 2015
BY: GWEN COLLINS- WOMACK.
ALL RIGHTS RESERVED. NO PART OF THIS BOOK MAY BE REPRODUCED, SCANNED, OR DISTRIBUTED IN ANY PRINTED OR ELECTRONIC FORM WITHOUT PERMISSION. PLEASE DO NOT PARTICIPATE IN OR ENCOURAGE PIRACY OF COPYRIGHTED MATERIALS IN VIOLATION OF THE AUTHOR'S RIGHTS. PURCHASE ONLY AUTHORIZED EDITIONS.

ISBN: 978-0-9829326-8-1

EDITED BY:
ANDRE RICARDO –
WWW.ANDRERICARDO.COM

PUBLISHED BY:
M. PUBLICATIONS LLC.
P.O BOX 327
ROANOKE, TX 76262
WWW.MPUBLICATIONS.COM

DEDICATION

I WOULD LIKE TO DEDICATE THIS BOOK TO:

WEST, MY LOVING HUSBAND, I SAY THANK YOU FOR LOVING ME IN SPITE OF ME.

TO MY CHILDREN PEDRA AND WARREN FOR SHARING ME WITH MANY AND LOVING ME NO MATTER WHAT.

ALL OF MY CHILDREN: FOR SUPPORTING ME AND SOMETIMES DRIVING ME CRAZY.

TO MY BROTHERS AND SISTERS: FOR LOVING ME THROUGH ADVERSITY.

TO MY PASTOR, BISHOP T.D. JAKES: FOR THE SERMONS THAT KEPT ME ALIVE DURING SOME VERY DARK MOMENTS.

TO MY MOTHER, LILA MAE: FOR BEING THE STRONG WOMAN THAT I NOW REALIZE SHE WAS.

FINALLY, **FOR ALL** WHO WOULD READ MY STORY AND PERHAPS MAY EVEN CATCH A GLIMPSE OF YOURSELF. I PRAY YOU BE BLESSED.

THIS IS FOR YOU.

THE EDITOR'S PREFACE

This is a serial memoir.

A memoir told in the third-person as opposed to a first-person account, because no one comes into existence without a history that precedes it.

And, this is a Journey.

A journey made by unbelievable choices. It's equal parts Tom Sawyer-- small town kid who innocently (and sometimes, cynically) gets into childhood mischief and Maya Angelou—strong-willed, independent woman whose daring personality and temerity sets her against the underground social networks of urban towns in Kentucky and West Virginia from the 1950's through the 1990's and beyond.

In this volume, you'll meet her grandmother, Cecil, a legatee of religious scholars and teachers and a pillar of the community.

Her mother, Lila Mae, a woman psychologically trapped between what is good for her and what she thinks is good for her. Also, one whose choice of men sets the stage for her daughter.

And, then... there's... "Jink." One of the most notorious men a woman could ever meet.

Sit back. This wild ride is just about to begin....

CHAPTER

"*Are you okay in there, Gwendolyn?*" The voice asked.

"Yeah, I got a lot to get out of me. It's gonna' take some time," said Gwen.

She urinated as fast as possible as she fought this sinking feeling of fear that started to paralyze her. But she mustered enough energy to ignore it. When their voices got lower, Gwen very slowly lifted herself off the commode and quietly tiptoed to the edge of the door, hoping that the sound of her getting up wouldn't draw their attention.
She leaned into the crack of the door when she heard Robert whispering to Wally. Picking up only a few words clearly, she heard Robert tell Wally,

"Let's just get that bitch! Let's tie her up and take her outback. We can have it set up before she comes out.

Instantly paralyzed, fear began to grip her as she knew they were talking about her. Shutting her eyes for a few moments, she tried to think of what to do. The only thing she came up with was to run. Gwen waited until there was an opportune time to make her escape but she didn't know exactly how.

Suddenly she heard the back door open and footsteps walking down the hallway towards a backroom. There was a lot of rumbling and things falling on the floor. She peeked back through the crack and didn't see anyone in her small view. So she opened the bathroom door and closed it softly, leaving the light on. She crept to the front door and again opened it and closed it softly. When she saw that she had made it safely out of the house, she jumped off the porch and ran straight into the dark field directly in front of Robert Lee's house.

She had gone about 400 to 500 feet before she heard the sound of the men running out of the house calling her name. As she ran deeper and deeper into the woods, she could hear things rustling around her, the sounds of wild dogs and boars in the vicinity were familiar to her. The voices screaming out her name were getting louder and closer. She knew she had to keep running as fast as she could now as the men begin to scream threats on her life and now her family.

CHAPTER

  Faint, brittle chips of blue paint stretch across the top of the frame overhanging what used to be a gleaming white marquis.
It's greeting, graced in genteel southern charm, is almost lost against a cast of yellowed layers. Seated at the entrance of the town's bridge, sometimes hidden by draping branches or mud-splattered weekends, it has remained quietly resilient for almost one hundred years:

Welcome to Madisonville
Population, 17,500

"That sign over there, you see it?"
"Which one are you talking about, Miss Barbara?"

"That old sign!"

Cecil looked to her right as Barbara took her hand off the steering wheel to point out the sign.

"You know, Cecil, I think we're very lucky to live where we live? Don't you think?"

Taken off guard by the question, Cecil says,

"I haven't given it much thought, but I reckon it's so. What makes you say that, Miss Barbara?"

"Well, I was just thinking about what happened last night to Nat King Cole. I don't know if you were paying any attention to the radio today when you were cleaning."

"I did hear something about him having to go to the hospital for something... but that was it."

"Well... it seems that he was having a concert in Birmingham and some three men rushed up on the stage and just attacked him. They knocked him down from his seat at the piano and they must have kicked over the microphone because from what we're told, when that thing hit the floor, it sounded like an explosion. Well, those men dragged him from the stage and they tried to either kidnap him or kill him. Luckily for him that the police were there to catch those men."

Cecil sat quiet. The drive across town from Miss Barbara's house to her home was a forty-five minute drive during rush hour. She thought about Nat King Cole for a second, but her mind went to the obituary she remembered she needed to type up for Sister Lorraine who had just passed away last Sunday. Cecil quickly put her thought on hold, knowing she had one more house to clean before she'd go to church tonight.

"Lord, I hope he's alright. That's why we don't play that rock and roll stuff in my house. That kind of music is of the devil and no good can come of it. You listen to that music then all of sudden you find yourself doin' things you never thought you'd do."

Barbara waited a moment to allow that sentiment to fade from their presence.

"Well, my husband and I are big fans of his. Just last week, my husband told me that he read something about Nat going on a trip to Cuba to record another album."

There was no motion from Cecil.

"Well, Cecil when was the last time you heard from your son?"

Cecil's eyes suddenly dilated.

"Ahh... mmm...well Miss Barbara... I can't say. It's been.... it's been," looking at Barbara but not seeing her. "I don't know how long it's been."

She turned to the other side trying not to think about the question anymore. Her eyes followed the row of houses as Barbara steadily cruised through the quiet neighborhood. She always knew when she was getting closer to home because the houses began to get a little smaller. Her mind began to think about her son again. Disappointment resounded in her voice when she said,

"Jack never calls. Never wrote to tell us where he is or how he's doing. My husband and I never understood what we could have done to make him hate us the way he does. All we know is that he lives in New York... in some part called, Brooklyn."

Barbara felt bad about Cecil's situation with her son, so she quickly changed the subject about Jack and asked about Lila.

"And, how's Lila Mae doing?"

"She's doing fine. I keep her at home to take care of my grandkids but she's taken up sewing now to keep her mind occupied. Hopefully, it could get her a job someplace, of course when the kids are old enough to go to school and come home by themselves."

"That's wonderful... and, how old are they now?"

"Let me see... Michael Douglas just turned five and Gwendolyn Faye is three. She'll be four in July."

"Listen, Cecil. I know things are tight but if you ever need anything, please don't hesitate to ask. I wanna' help. I've been there myself. When I had my eldest, no one ever thought I'd amount to something. Even my parents were ashamed of me. You tell Lila when she's ready, she can come by the house and we can find some work for her. We could always use extra help around the house every now and then, especially when we have our weekend parties."

"That's very kind of you, Miss Barbara. But, I think right now, I just rather her be at home taking care of the kids for now. But we'll see.

On the hill, just above the Collins' home, an older woman was watering her flowers when her eyes met with Barbara. Barbara slowed down and pulled over in front of her house. Mrs. Delores Dunn took off her bright green gardening gloves and walked over to Barbara's car.

"Well, good afternoon or should I say good early evening, you two!" Mrs. Dunn said, as she now noticed Cecil sitting in the passenger's seat.

Cecil extends her hand out the window while Barbara smiles,

"Good afternoon, Ms. Delores! What a beautiful afternoon this is!"

"Ms. Cecil, just this morning, Mr. Dunn asked me if I heard how you and your family were doing. We had heard about the fire at your house last week."

"We're doing just fine, praise the Lord" Cecil said as she gripped Mrs. Dunn hand a bit firmer.

"My husband told me that he heard from the men down at the gas station that you had lost everything."

"No, we lost some things. We had a brush fire and the kitchen window was open. One of the kitchen curtains had gotten untied and was hanging outside the window when a flame caught it. We have some damage to the kitchen and a few presents that I had been hiding for my grand babies; they were lost but nothing that we can't fix."

Delores wiped her hand on her apron and looked at Barbara,

"Miss Barbara, can you wait a second. I'm coming right back, I forget to get something."

Delores walked quickly inside the house. She came back with a bag with something unusually large on the inside. Delores reached the car and adjusted her reading glasses while handing the bag to Cecil.

"Miss Delores, what is this?" said Cecil curiously.

"Miss Cecil, you know when you have kids you always need something for them to play with. This was my youngest daughter's doll. She just went off to school and hadn't played with this for years."

She exhaled and put her hand on Cecil arm.

"Miss Cecil, please take it for your granddaughter. I think my daughter called it a "Wedding Doll." It has some significance but I have not idea about that. And, I'm sorry I don't have anything for your son, we'll make sure to have something for him next time okay.

"Oh, Ms. Delores, you don't have to. Those kids get into enough trouble as it is."

"No, Cecil, it's really no trouble, please take it."

Cecil was silent for a moment and gradually accepted the package.

"This means a lot to me. Thank you for remembering my grandchildren. Have a good night now, ya' hear". Cecil said as Barbara slowly began to move on.

CHAPTER 3

"Cecil, the pastor needs you to help him with the final edit of his acceptance speech and he needs to meet the printer's deadline in an hour!" A frantic woman was leaning into a doorway in front of Cecil. With Cecil's hand on the typewriter, she is momentarily distracted from her typing; the letters on the paper seemed blurry. She couldn't make out what she was typing nor remember exactly what it was she was trying to say.

Before she was even able to rub her eyes, a voice in front of her screams, "Cecil, come quick, there's someone on the phone looking for you. She says there's been a fire at the house and they can't find Lila and the kids, you have to go home now!"

Oh, sweet Jesus, Cecil thought as she struggled to push her chair back and get her balance. 'No, not another fire, not again.'

"Cecil... Cecil... Thank God you're here!" In the doorway now stood, Barbara. She was as pale as a ghost and fraught with desperation. "Cecil, thank God I found you. I need your help desperately! We have visitors; my husband's relatives came down from Louisville. We must have breakfast made quickly. I tried to put something together but it just wouldn't do. Cecil, it'll just be for a few hours, I promise you'll be off by 6 tonight. Cecil, you must come, don't just stand there."

Before Cecil could respond, she looked around her to grab her bag. When she raised her head, all three women were standing in the hallway screaming out her name, each demanding that she come with them.

"Mama... Mama!" Lila said softly as she gently tugged on Cecil's shoulder. *"Wake up, mama!"*

Cecil opened her eyes to a blur of color and a familiar smell.

"Mama, Misses Linney is calling you. I think you have a phone call."
"Okay... alright, tell Misses Linney, I'll be right there."

It took a few moments for Cecil to get her bearings. She found herself lying down on the couch in the living room. She remembered sitting down on the couch after coming home from work late last night. The blurred image of her daughter walking out the front door led her to turn around and look at the clock on the side of the couch.

It was 9:30 am. Noticing the lateness of the time, she started talking to herself. "Oh, my Lord, I'm late, I have to go to Miss Barbara's today. Oh, Lord, look at me I can't go in looking like this! I need a bath and I have to make these kids their lunch for school."

She forced herself to sit up straight by reaching for the table in front of her to help her to lean up. Then something dawned on her: it's

Saturday! 'Oh my Lord', she thought to herself. She eased herself back down on the couch trying to figure out what all she had to do today. Then she remembered she promised another family that she'd clean their house after their party. Afterwards, she had choir rehearsal and an Ushers board meeting for tomorrow's services.

"*Mama!*" She heard in a distance, *"telephone."*
"I'm coming! Hold on a minute."

Cecil left the couch and walked to the bathroom, noticing the door slightly ajar. She was about to knock but very gently pushed the door just wide enough to see if someone was there. From that sliver of an opening, she saw Gwen standing on a milk crate looking at herself in the mirror. Gwen would turn from the left to the center to the right. She would even try to see how she looked from behind. Cecil had to stifle a laugh when she noticed Gwen trying to look down her own blouse and puff her chest out while smiling at herself in the mirror.

Cecil very carefully pulled the door as close to being shut as quietly as possible. She crept a few steps back until she was some distance away to where she could walk hard enough for Gwen to hear her coming. As she looked at Gwen looking at herself in the mirror, the memory of Gwen's birth came rushing back to her as if it were just yesterday.

***

"It's a girl!" Cecil remembers herself saying to Lila as she laid in the bed just after delivery. Lila had passed out just at that very moment. Cecil said it again, this time acknowledging anyone within hearing distance. "You have a baby girl. I'll call and let everybody know," she said. As she made her way down the hall of the clinic to the phone booth, she nearly tripped over the empty wheel chairs that lined the walls.

She fumbled to find a nickel in her purse as she unraveled a small, crumpled piece of paper with a phone number written on it. Her hands slightly shaking, she dials the number. *"Hello, is Charles there?"* The voice on the other end confirmed what she already knew in her heart. *"Well, if you see or hear from him, tell him he is a daddy now."*

He was nowhere to be found. There was no need to telephone anyone else she knew. Her daughter Lila would only want to reach him. "I tried to tell that girl to stay away from him," she muttered to herself as she walked back to the small room where Lila was resting after five long hours of intense labor. Finally, that part was over!

Lila was waiting for the nurse to return with the baby. She looked around at the gray walls in the tiny room, starkly furnished with only two straight-back chairs, and a metal nightstand in the corner. She pulled the thin blanket up around her neck, closed her eyes, slid down in the bed and ached for Charles. She had hoped Charles would be sitting at her bedside when they brought in their baby -- clean and powdered and wriggly. I wonder where Charles could be, she thought. Doesn't he care about me?

Hours later, when she opened her eyes again, she saw the doctor standing over her dressed in his wrinkled, blue scrubs. The nurse walked in and stood right behind him while holding a tiny little bundle in her hands.

"Is that her?" Lila asked. "Is that my baby? Please let me hold her."

Looking down at the beautiful little girl she had just brought into the world, she desperately wanted everything to be all right.

"If all goes well, Ms. Oldham, you can go home in three days," the

doctor said.

"Thank you so much, doctor, but I am ready to go now."

Lila was excited about that tiny pink squirming baby, but she felt the pain of a widening wound because Charles had not been there with her to see his child born. She felt as if her world was crashing down around her. She looked at Cecil and despite the fact that she was overjoyed, she knew her mother was disappointed in her. She knew the sacrifice that her mother was making for her. She thought of the argument she overheard that her mom and dad had just a few weeks prior about this pregnancy. Lila could only hope that her father's threat to leave was just in the heat of the moment. She remembered her mom's words, "She's the only one we got left...and, I won't abandon my baby."

Lila knew Cecil didn't want her to bring yet another life into this world out of wedlock. She always heard Cecil telling her that there's a much bigger world outside of their small town but she would need an education to make it out there. "You're going to college, young lady and make something of yourself. Make us proud!" That was the refrain she heard almost all of her life. Now, at eighteen, she made the exact same mistake Cecil made when she was a teenager.

***

"Nurse, has anyone called me?"

"No, there have been no calls for you, Ms. Oldham, since the last time you asked. Why don't you lay back and get some rest," the nurse said.

Lila sensed both kindness and pity in her voice. As the tears streamed down her cheeks, Lila turned her head to the wall and softly cried herself to sleep. Hours later, Lila awoke to the sound of the nurse entering the room.

"Breakfast time, Ms. Oldham."
"I'm not hungry."

Lila turned away from the nurse now facing the wall. She began to reminisce about the private moments she shared with Charles and all of the I-love-you's and sweet promises that he would make to her someday and buy a house for her and Michael to live in while he kissed her passionately. That pleasurable fantasy abruptly ended when she realized he wouldn't be there for her, much less her children. She gagged as she motioned frantically for the nurse to get the bedpan from the metal table. Lila lurched forward over the dirty-looking metal bowl as it was slid to her. When there was no more left in her stomach to spill out, she laid back on the pillow again. The aftertaste of vomit in her mouth caused her to gag again. The nurse handed her the room temperature cup of water that was on the table, while tapping her forehead with a cool washcloth for a few seconds before she left.

Lila's thoughts raced through her mind as she stirred uneasily in the bed. She remembered living this moment once before with her firstborn, Michael. It was as if she had just duplicated his birth all over again. The nurse shuffled in carrying a stack of crisp white sheets and interrupted Lila's anxious thoughts.

"What a beautiful baby you have!" The nurse chirped a little too cheerfully. *"Is this your first?"*

Lila heard the question, but hurt choked back the answer.

"No, this is my second. I have a little boy. He's two years old," she mumbled sorrowfully.

"Your husband must be so proud to have a boy and a girl," said

the nurse.

    Lila could not answer for the lump in her throat. It was only the rustle of the sheets that broke the awkwardness of that silent moment. That statement made Lila think about her life. As she nestled into the newly fresh sheets, she began to visualize her current situation. Her innocence and her youth all seem to be passing by right before her eyes. As the nurse continued to clean up the room, she wondered if she would ever get married to anyone. She was in this same position two years before. What makes this any different from the last time? She asked herself. What lessons did she learn when Michael' Sr. abandoned his newborn son? These were the questions Lila never dared to ask herself for fear of the reality of the answer.

    Lila dropped out of school a couple of years ago. She hadn't even finished her junior year. Now, with her little boy and a newborn baby girl, what was she to do? She leaned up and sat upright on her bed after the nurse had left the room. She looked around and saw Cecil, her mom, fast asleep holding her baby. Lila knew she would do whatever it took to take care of her growing family.

***

    As a single tear ran down Cecil's face, she remembered that those were some hard times for her and her husband. But as she thought about the love she had for Lila and the kids, she took a deep breath and said to herself, Ahhh', my grandbaby ain't so much a baby anymore. She's growing up so fast. Lord knows I love my family and these precious grandkids and I would do anything in the world for them.

CHAPTER

Michael got up first. He always slept closest to the wall, and Gwen, she slept on the side closest to the window. Michael liked to get up on his own without any help from above. This often meant that he had to shrug Gwen awake.

"Gwen... Gwen... let's go get some cereal and wait for Mr. Charlie outside!"

"Ahhh... I wanna' sleep... leave me alone."

"Gwen, wake up. I saw Granny hide that new cereal in the cabinet."

Michael shook Gwen until she leaned up. She sluggishly crawled out of the bed and slid into her slippers that were sprawled by a small table on the other side of the room. As they slowly walked out the door, competing scents vied for their attention. Michael and Gwen zeroed in on the scrambled eggs, ham and homemade biscuits. And, as was usual with Granny, her beautiful voice was singing one of the songs she'd always sing before the congregation. As they walked closer to the kitchen, they noticed Granny holding both of her hands up toward the ceiling as she sang:

> "Then sings my soul, my Saviour God, to Thee,
> How great Thou art, how great Thou art!
> Then sings my soul, my Saviour God, to Thee,
> How great Thou art, how great Thou art!
>
> "When through the woods and forest glades I wander
> and hear the birds sing sweetly in the trees;
> when I look down from lofty mountain grandeur,
> and hear the brook, and feel the gentle breeze..."

"Well, good morning sleepy heads; how are you this morning?"

"I'm fine, granny," said Michael as he threw himself on one of the kitchen table chairs.

It wasn't a very large kitchen; in fact it was rather small. It shared its space with a small nook that was used for the laundered clothes and those that needed to be ironed. Cecil never let that nook get piled up though. We never thought anything about the space, we were just used to it. It wasn't odd to ever see Granny ironing our clothes in the kitchen. No one ever really complained either, it was a benefit to iron while the smell of succulent herbs and spices of granny's cooking often filled the air. Gwen merely rubbed her eyes and slowly sat on the chair opposite of him.

"Gwendolyn Faye, cat caught your tongue," Cecil inquired, barely looking up from the piles of clothes that sat on the edge of the ironing board.

Cecil had one of those old cast-iron irons with a withered electrical chord on the end that had been wrapped with black electrical tape too many times over. Nevertheless, the most recent layer now unraveling. There was always a big can of spray starch nearby to spray on the clothes before she pressed into them. When she sprayed it, it would always remind Michael and Gwen of speckled snowflakes on a Christmas tree. But, it was no holiday when walking through the kitchen meant nearly suffocating due to a cloud of starchy smoke. The kids always knew that smell, it would seep into their room early in the morning where they knew that granny was home, probably had breakfast done, the garbage put out and had nearly finished ironing the family's clothes...all before 7:30 a.m.

***

"Good mornin' " a groggy Gwen said as she continue to rub her eyes.

"Your breakfast is in the oven. Don't eat any of that cold cereal until after you had something nutritional in your tummies. You hear me?"

They both answered in unison,

"Yes, granny."

"Did the both of you brush your teeth and wash your face?"

Cecil was insistent of this even with her own children.

"Yes, granny," said Michael, as he reached for the box of Sugar Frosted Flakes. *"See!"*

Michael flashed a grin with one of his front teeth still waiting to grow back in. His smile always made her laugh. A few seconds passed when

Cecil looked toward Gwen and asked,

> "Gwendolyn Faye, did you brush your teeth, yet?"
> "No, ma'am."
> "Young lady, get yourself to the bathroom and don't come back until you're finished"

Gwen slowly got up from the table and the sound of her well-worn slippers dragged over the freshly mopped floor leaving streaks that aroused Cecil's frustration.

> "Child, pick up your feet when you walk, you're dirtying my clean floor.

As Gwen reached the kitchen doorway, she heard her grandmother's voice.

> "Where's your mother?"

Cecil said with a tone of resignation. She would shake a freshly pressed shirt before draping it over a hanger.

"I don't know, granny," said Gwen, not knowing whether to continue or wait for further instruction.

Stretching out a long pair of pants and pouring water on it, Cecil, measuring out the legs,

> "*Tell your mom I need to talk to her.*"

Gwen walked to each of the rooms, knocking while gently pushing the door to see if her mother was asleep. Nothing. She was about to walk back to the kitchen when she heard a canister fall in the back of the house. She walked through the narrow hallway to see Lila sitting on the step that leads to the backyard, tapping a new box of Pall Mall cigarettes in her free palm.

"Momma, granny's calling you."

"Okay, dear. Tell her I'll be there in a minute." As Gwen was about to walk off, "Gwendolyn, do me a favor. Go to the stove and light this for me," handing her a newly drawn cigarette. "Don't put it in your mouth, just light it and come right back."

"Yes, momma."

A few minutes had passed when Lila remembered about the cigarette. As she turned to call Gwen, she looked up to find Cecil standing at the backdoor.

***

Cecil was old, old school. Her portly frame stood about 5'9" tall and was probably 170 lbs. if it were possible for her to wear all of her clothes at the same time. She always wore her hair pinned back that accentuated her angular face. As far as anyone knew, Cecil came from a generation of Oldhams, black Kentuckians, that went back long past the Jim Crow era. But, Cecil was strikingly exotic. A beautiful woman whose coffee-with-cream-colored skin, piercing eyes, long-narrowed nose and thin lips could have easily passed for a Native American.

***

She stood there wiping her free hand on her weather-beaten apron with embroidered apples on it and she leaned over giving Lila Mae the cigarette she took from Gwen.

"Baby, you have to stop this. This is no good for you. This is unbecoming of a child of God."

"Momma, I promise I'll quit."

"You shouldn't be smoking in front of these kids, either. You don't *know what they're putting in these things."*

There was no reply but this wasn't the first time Cecil had spoken to Lila about her habits. But as usual, she left it alone, hoping that Lila would know how much she cared about her. At that very moment, both women heard a knock on the front door and a pattering of footsteps racing toward it.

***

Each house has its own personality and every house communicates with its owners. It tells you in subtle ways, what it needs and when its satisfied. This was particularly true when it came to guests showing up and especially unexpectedly.

***

Within a moment's time they heard the children talking with someone, then the door closed. The footsteps of the kids faded in one direction while the sound of heels echoes closer and closer to the backdoor.

"Why, good morning! What have we here? A prayer meeting or a cigarette break?"

"Gladys, you know how to make an entrance!" Cecil commented while shaking her head.

"Good morning, Aunt Gladys." said Lila as she exhaled a drag away from her, now holding the cigarette behind her back.

"Maybe," said Cecil, "you can talk to this girl about this thing she's doing. I know it's all the rave and all of her friends are doing it, but I can't help but to think there's something wrong about this."

"Cecil, child, she'll grow out of it the way she did with her training bra," said Gladys as she now set her attention to Lila. *"Lila Mae... you really need to think about what you want to do with your life. And,*

what's this I hear you got a new man?"

"New man?"

Cecil looked at Lila amazed. Lila said nothing but looked down and stepped on the cigarette with the edge of her old, crumpled slipper.

"When were you going to tell me? "

"I...I didn't know how to tell you." Lila said softly. *"How did you find out Aunt Gladys?"*

"Girl," Gladys said as she put her hand on her waist. "*I don't have to go no place to find out anything. You know when I'm outside pulling up my tomatoes, Mrs. Gilliam would bring over some apples and girl, she'd just have to tell me what Sister Williams told her at the Laundromat. Well, child, I tell ya', when I tell ya', when I tell ya' what Mrs. Smith told Sister Williams the other night at--"*

"Who's Mrs. Smith, I don't think I know her?" Cecil replied. "Wait... wait a minute... is that the short woman with the big nose? That's the woman who tried to steal all her family's inheritance after her mother died?"

"Girl, that's the one. She has a sister who lives in Texas with her two daughters and one of them is married to the preacher...Well, Mrs. Smith told Sister Williams that she overheard this guy in the supermarket talking about how he was doing this and doing that with the daughter of this minister who sings in the choir and writes the obituaries for the church. Girl, I just knew he was referring to this young woman right here."

Cecil said nothing as she stared at Lila for a moment. She turned around from standing in the doorway and slowly walked back inside and down the hallway into the living room. She walked in front of the window and parted the drapes. She looked at Michael and Gwen playing in the front yard. Her attention focused on Gwen for a moment.

  Gwen was playing by herself as Michael and some neighborhood boys played marbles and hide-n-go seek. Gwen was there twirling and doing cartwheels and before long she had a pretend-microphone in her hand, singing to an imaginary audience. Cecil took her eyes off of Gwen for a moment and noticed the other neighbors sitting outside on the porch. They too were looking at Gwen and smiling and speaking to one another. Cecil took a few steps over to the couch, sat down and picked up the family bible that laid on the coffee table. This was her place of respite.

CHAPTER 5

Amazing Grace
How sweet the sound
That saved a wretch like me
I once was lost, but now I'm found
Was blind, but now I see...

'Twas grace that taught my heart to fear
And grace, my fears relieved;
How precious did that grace appear
The hour I first believed...

***

There was no greater force that connected a community within the south than the church. This was particularly true for African-Americans. There were no personal or communal activities that didn't involve the church in some way whether it were local politicians wanting support for a certain legislation or an individual pursuing public office: the church was always a forum to get your message out.

In Madisonville, much like the rest of Kentucky, two denominations held sway over much of the area's population: the Baptists and the Methodists. Kentucky has the unusual distinction of having both the president of the Confederacy, Jefferson Davis and the president of the United States, Abraham Lincoln to call Kentucky their birthplace. It would seem, however, that the church would be theoretically opposed to the idea of slavery but this was not the case.

Like the nation, the Baptists split into two main divisions the Baptist (Northern Admin.) and the Southern Baptist (Convention.) For those African-Americans who wanted autonomous control and direction over their services and content, appointed leaders from within the African-American constituents of the larger body of the church. Who appealed to the clergy for a separation to form their own legally recognized church. With the exception of the formation of The First African Baptist [nee: First Colored Baptist] Church of Savannah in 1777 and a scattering of individual and independent Black churches over the next 40 years, this post-Antebellum movement marked the beginning of the modern Black church in America.

The Black Church became for all intents and purposes a de facto government where it dealt with issues that affected its parishioners by organizing councils to deal with education, jobs and work-related issues as well as housing.

It was a place where individuals would gather to barter and donate services. And, during moments of social conflict: it was a refuge from aggression and conflict. To local authorities, the black church was the voice of their community. It was a place where everyone greeted you with a title whether it was Mr. or Mrs. or Dr. or Mrs., you were well respected and heard. Whatever social position you had in the community, for many people, your achievements or social contributions didn't amount to much in their eyes. But in church, who you were thought of outside didn't matter, you could be a doctor or a janitor. What mattered was that you were there.

The church during that time was a place where you could be somebody. It was, and still is for many families the center of African-American life and one of the positive historically defining characteristics of people.

***

The front doors to the Oak Grove Baptist Church, just adjacent to a rusted frame with the church's name and greeting, opened and closed constantly as members and children dragging their feet behind them, played out the same routine every Sunday: week after week; season after season.

Inside, the lobby housed crowds as people walked in different directions. Some walked into the sanctuary, some stood and chatted with friends, while others passed the time looking for something to distract them. The scene resembled a very busy train station.

Placards and commendations above the lobby doors decorated the purple and red felt-covered wall. If one were to stand just a few feet away from the sanctuary's door, rainbow waves of wide pastel- colored brimmed or "cloche" hats revealed as much about the woman as the shoes she wore. For it was on these hats that telltale ornaments like knots or flowers or arrows told whether she was available, married or taken. The men beside them wore modest two-piece suits, straight leg gabardines that narrowed as it reached the ankle. Some men wore the pants length to a slight break at the collar of the shoe or just above the ankle. Men also wore without exception black or dark brown lace up's. Few also sported the wingtip design. Being appropriately dressed for Sunday service was as protocol as the fresh flowers that decorated the base of the pulpit.

The church honored dignitaries like pastors, benevolent contributors, political servants or long-time members with framed pictures on the wall and a brief description of thanks. Members like Sara Phillips Martin who's work in the church, as a school teacher and a choir member was remembered for decades, especially for her quiet acts of selflessness and kindness to everyone she met.

Mrs. Martin passed on her love of family, church, service to others and a need for education to her daughter, Cecil. And, it was this community that surrounded Sara with love, as the church bulletin stated, "Went home to be with The Lord."

A broad, but unspoken code-of-conduct however was strictly adhered to: the Church was no place to discuss one's real private life that was to be played out in *grown folks* homes. So, it came as some shock and embarrassment when a few short months later, Cecil learned that her teenage daughter, Lila Mae was pregnant.

She had done the exact same thing at that time of her life. Cecil made a promise to herself and to God that she'd help her daughter overcome the hardships of being a single mother she was likely to face.

***

As the door opened to the sanctuary, the Reverend Doctor Johnston had just started the sermon, *Jacob and Esau*.

"Isaac, praise the Lord, as we all know had Jacob. And, we know-" looking around the congregation, "we all *should* know, brothers and sisters, that Jacob a descendent from Abraham would be the one that would carry on the lineage... I said, lineage!" (A few members of the congregation yelled out "Amen!") "It would be through his lineage that would give birth to the Messiah. Can I get an Amen?"

Loud voices were heard all over the room, "Thank you, Jesus, Praise The Lord!"

"But", Pastor Johnston wiping his forehead with a handkerchief he took from his breast pocket. "But, what about Esau? I said, what about Esau? (There was silence) Esau, brothers and sisters was Isaac's son too. Now, don't leave him out of the story, now. We shouldn't forget him anymore than... than any parent would forget the name of their first child. Can you imagine having kids and, ... and, some of you are veterans at making babies... but can you imagine having all these kids and you don't remember the first time you became a parent? No, brothers and sisters, we don't and Isaac didn't, either."

"Preach on, pastor! Preach on!" said one excited lady in the third row.

"Esau, I said, Esau was a man on the outs'! Now, you may be saying, why was he on the outs', pastor? He had a good home, good food, couldn't ask for a better father. But Esau was on the outs' because he lived outside. He ate outside. He thought outside. You could say he lived and thought outside the box. Esau hunted and ate big game, big goats, cows and big meats. But, what didn't he do? Esau never brought any of that big game home; he brought the scraps. Can I hear an amen?"

"Amen, pastor, amen!" the crowd, roared.

"Looking at the collection plate this morning, there are few Esau's out there in the pew. Brothers and Sisters, Esau was a loner... a private person who didn't care much for others. Can I hear someone say, loner?"

"Loner!"

"Do you know what happens when you're a loner? When you make decisions without regard to anyone else, without thinking how I use my advantage to help more than myself? When you fall... and we all fall, at some point in our lives... when you fall you don't have someone whom you nourished to help you back up..."

Pastor Johnston continued in this line for some time unaware of rustling in the choir section.

In the choir stand, directly behind the pulpit, Cecil looked around from left to right, sometimes looking behind her as Pastor Johnston continued his sermon. It was unusual for Lila not to be near Cecil, but somehow Cecil didn't notice Lila's absence during the worship service.

Mrs. Brown, an elderly woman, who sang in the choir when Sara and her were very young, pointed to the door to the left. This was the door the choir used to come in through.

Cecil did the unusual thing, she tiptoed out of the choir and quietly made her way to the exit without letting Pastor Johnston know of her passage. She walked through the small dressing room that led to the lobby. There she found Lila alone on a bench weeping in her hands.

"What are you doing here?" Cecil said as she sat down next to Lila.
"Momma, I can't go back in there?"
"Why? What's the matter? You can tell me, it's going to be all right, you hear? Now, tell momma what's the matter."

It was a moment before Lila could get herself together to speak without the tears streaming down her face.

"Momma... I just can't."
"Child, why... what happened. Did someone threaten you?"
"No, momma. It's nothing like that."

Lila rubbed her eyes with a hanky and inhaled a big breath. On the exhale she said,

"Momma, I'm a failure. That's why daddy left us. It's because of me. Because I had these two kids and I didn't marry either of the fathers."
"No!" Cecil was emphatic. " No, it's not child. Don't say that! Your daddy needed some time to straighten out a few things."
"If he needed to straighten out a few things, why did he take all of his clothes?"
"Lila, he needs some space to clear his head. That's all there is to it. I just spoke to him yesterday and I'm going to visit him soon. So don't you go worrying yourself about him."

Cecil looked at the sorry on her face and was disturbed by the impression on her heart.

"Is this all you have to tell me?" There was silence. "Child, open your mouth and talk to me. I said is there something you need to tell me?"

"Momma, I think I'm pregnant."

"Pregnant!" Cecil was besides herself.

"Momma, I'm so sorry, I've been wanting to tell you but there wasn't a good time."

"Oh, Lord, not again!"

Cecil stood up and paced around back and forth mumbling the word until she slowly came back.

"Momma, I'm sorry, I didn't know it would happen."

"We had to stop choir rehearsal the other night because someone made a comment about a girl named, Goree. One man said he had this girl doing this and that and had her over here and over there and doing all kinds of things in his car but when he called out her name this other guy came running over and punched him in the stomach. Oh Lord, that was terrible." Turning to Lila, "Please tell me he's not a married man."

"No, momma. It's Abram. Abram White, you know, the guy who normally sits at the end of the row."

"Oh, I know him. He's the one with the white buck shoes and the greasy hair."

Cecil looked at her daughter and the dark mascara lines on both sides of her face. She remembered the isolation she felt just before she told her mother. But this time, there wasn't any excuse. She was going to have to find a way to get married and take care of her responsibilities. That's what she promised Sara just before she died.

"Okay, I'm going tell you what we're going to do."

Cecil stood up and took Lila's hands into hers and gently lifted her up to stand.

"From now on, I'm going to treat you like an adult first and my daughter second. Tell Romeo that I want to meet him and I want him to be prepared to tell me how he's going to take care of his child. Do you hear me?"

"Yes, momma."

"Now, I'm going to tell you what my mother told me when I told her I was pregnant with you. Take five minutes to cry and let it all out. Let everything out. Then I want you to put on some of this lipstick, fix your dress and put on those high-heeled shoes and go and meet the world. It's about time you showed the world a new face. Lila Mae, I'm not going to baby you anymore."

"Yes, momma."

"I'm going back inside now. I expect to see you walking back in there in 4:45 seconds from now. You understand?"

"Yes, momma."

"When you come walking through that door, I'd better see the new Lila Mae."

"Yes, momma."

CHAPTER

"Gwendolyn... Gwendolyn...Gwendolyn Faye..." There was an even longer pause as Lila was reaching down under her bed looking for one of her sandals. "Gwendolyn Faye, where are you?" Lila walked to her bedroom door with one shoe on and one in her hand, she pried the door to the children's bedroom open. "Gwendolyn Faye?"

The house was quiet except for the clicking sound of the second hand that made its strenuous march up the latter half of the hour. She walked to the living room and looked out the window. She heard a faint noise coming from outside but even with the drapes parted; she couldn't make out whom it was. Lila walked on to the patio and walked past two rocking chairs that her mom and dad sat on when she was just a kid. She remembered many times her father calling her to come in from this chair. She stopped for a moment and realized that she's an adult now and about to call for Gwen in the same way. To think she was behaving like her father puzzled her.

Leaning over the railing, she saw a crowd of children walking around. Charlie Hassett, an elderly man, was reaching in his pocket and handing something to one little kid. He had a large sack that he usually used to carry the vegetables in his garden in. He unloaded the old bag and handed something to one child. Lila couldn't make out what it was. He dug back into his bag and handed something else to another kid. Every child seemed to by vying for what was in that bag. Lila noticed Gwen and Michael amongst the crowd as several kids tried to peek inside of the bag from the back. What was in that burlap bag she wondered. What were they hiding? She knew if she asked the kids, they wouldn't tell her the truth.

"Michael Douglas and Gwendolyn Faye, get home right now! Right now, you hear me!"

Michael and Gwen turned around immediately then turned back to Mr. Charlie before they took off running back to the house.

***

"Mr. Charlie," as he was respectfully known throughout the neighborhood, was something of an enigma. He had a wonderful vegetable garden where he grew all different kinds of produce to various vendors. Mr. Charlie lived on this block for several decades yet, no one knew anything about him and certainly never went over to his house. The extent of neighborly courtesy was a wave to him as he walked by followed by a grumbling about his appearance. Indeed, not even Lila knew anything about him. She never even heard a word spoken about him by her own parents.

Mr. Charlie had an outgrowth on his stomach, the result of an abdominal hernia. But, no one seemed to realize this until the bulge around his stomach got large enough as to move side to side across his already protruding stomach. The neighbors had always wondered what was wrong with him and why hadn't he seen a doctor about it. The neighbors were always whispering and gossiping about Mr. Charlie and the women he had. Their comments were harsh and endless.

Mr. Charlie was married to an obviously younger woman. Well, the neighbors didn't like that either. They would say vicious comments like, *Who was she? Where'd she come from? Do you see her hair? Oh my God, she looks like an alien. And, what's with that red hair? I heard there are people who paint their head red to worship the devil. Yeah, she looks like a heathen.* The cruel comments never ceased.

This woman with whom no one adult wanted to associate with, was named Imogene. The kids in the neighborhood never addressed her as Mrs. Hassett; she was simply referred to as "Fire Truck," alluding to a traumatic experience with a fire truck in her youth. The neighbors, however, privately laughed at this mock but none of them inquired the meaning of this appellation.

When she'd see the neighborhood kids crowd around Mr. Charlie, she'd run into the house and return with a broom to scare them off. From a distance, the kids would make loud wailing sounds of a fire truck in response. Mr. Charlie never said anything other then hello to his wife as he made his way inside. Mrs. Hassett, would stand at the door for a few moments and look around to see if there were any more brave souls who'd come to knock on the door.

***

This particular morning, Mr. Charlie had returned home very early. Maybe he had sold all the fruits and vegetables to one buyer and decided to come back home early. One of the neighborhood kids noticed him walking home and ran outside to meet him, then another and another until Mr. Charlie was surrounded by all of the neighborhood kids. Only the kids knew that Mr. Charlie had a bag full of candy and snacks. No one knew where he got it but he always had a bag of candy. "I got some Red Hots today and I got some Tuttii Fruitti..." and he'd call off names of candies he'd recognize from the partially torn wrappers that covered them.

Because it was a burlap sack that was always filled with vegetables, Mr. Charlie's candy bag often had a terrible smell, especially when he first opened it. Gwen pulled on her brother's shirt and pinched her nose with the other hand. Michael shrugged it off and went into his pocket and gave Mr. Charlie the nickel he asked for in exchange for the candy. Mr. Charlie smiled at Gwen and gave her a small bag of pop corn. He knew she'd like it.

"Here you go, little lady!" Mr. Charlie said as he touched her hand.

Gwen looked at him and said nothing, trying to distract her attention from the heavy scent of gasoline that permeated the popcorn.

"Michael Douglas and Gwendolyn Faye, get home right now! Right now, you hear me!"

Both Michael and Gwen turned around to see Lila leaning over the railing waving to them. They turned back around facing Mr. Charlie so they could stuff their mouth with the candies they just received. Michael and Gwen ran home as fast as they could. As they raced up the porch and into the house, each tried to dodge the soft flimsy, faded pink slipper that Lila swung at them.

"Didn't I tell you two that I don't want you leaving this house unless I or your grandma says it's okay?"

There was no response as both ran into the room and locked the door behind them. Lila knocked on the door.

"Michael Douglas and Gwendolyn Faye put on your clothes I want you to come to the store with me."

"*Momma, we want to stay home and play outside,*" said Gwen.

"Listen, I don't want you to back talk me young lady. Now, you and your brother get ready, I'm leaving in a few minutes and I need the both of you to help me carry the bags from the grocery store."

"*But, momma,*" Michael said, "*you said I could go to my daddy's house today.*"

Lila thought for a moment, and then realized that she did promise to let him go a couple of nights back.

"I know I said that, but I need you to help me with the groceries. I also have something to tell you two. So, I want you to come with me so we can talk. After we come back with the groceries, you can go to your daddy's house. Now the both of you hurry up, I have some other things to do today."

Usually when Lila or Cecil needed a small amount of groceries, they'd walk up the hill to the small convenience store. But when they needed to do "real" grocery shopping, they'd call for a taxi to go to Kroger's, which was about 15 minutes away.

This morning was different though; Lila needed an excuse to talk with her children but needed more time than the corner grocery store would allow her. So, they made off for Kroger's by foot.

"Momma, why are we walking to Kroger's, why don't we take the taxi?" Gwen wondered as she clutched her paper dolls.

"Walking is good, you need the exercise." Lila said as she looked straightway.

"But momma, it's such a long walk. I don't wanna go, it's too far" Gwen said as she stood still.

"Gwendolyn Faye, why do you like to backtalk me so much?"

Lila knew she needed to give them a better excuse because Gwen wasn't going to be appeased so easily. She stopped and turned to them,

"I asked you to come with me... because I need to talk to the both of you. I feel like I need to let you know something...."

Michael looked up,

"What is it, momma? Are you sick or something""

"No, no it's nothing like that. I... I'm getting married again."

Gwen and Michael looked at each other in shock.

"I know this is coming as a surprise but I'd rather you hear it from me then have to find out about it somewhere else," Lila said as she stooped down to look at her children. "I want you to know that everything's going to be just fine."

"Who is he, momma?" Michael said.

"His name is Abram. He's a friend of mine from church. We've been talking for awhile and we both love each other and we want to get married."

"Does this mean, we're going to have a new daddy?" said Gwen.

"Yes and he wants to meet you both. He wants to be friends with you." Lila knew that they weren't convinced. "He's coming over this afternoon and he's going to have dinner with us. So, Michael I need you to come home for dinner tonight to meet him."

Michael pouted and Gwen stared at the ground.

"Michael, after dinner you can go back to your grandmother's house but I don't want you to mention anything until I tell you it's okay. You hear me?"

"Yes, momma."

"Now that we have that settled, let's go and call a cab and go to the supermarket." Lila said as she searched in her pocketbook to separate some bills and to fish for some coins at the bottom of her bag.

"Momma," Gwen said softly, "does this mean that I have to divorce my real daddy?"

"No, dear, it doesn't mean that." Raising her head to look at Gwen, "It doesn't mean that at all."

CHAPTER 7

It didn't happen often, but there were times when either Cecil or Lila was at home. One day it happened and as in every incident, the rules of the house were suspended until either of them came home.

One morning Gwen had gotten up early and walked to the bedroom door where her slippers lay. As she opened the door, she heard Lila and Cecil talking about leaving, when they expected to be back home and who was going to leave the babysitting directions for Gwen.

It was clear from what Gwen heard that she'd have the day to herself. Cecil was going work and Lila was to run some errands, but what most intrigued Gwen was the brief discussion about a tray full of the chocolate chip cookies that Cecil had made earlier that morning for the church's bake sale. Gwen heard both women agree that the tray would not be safe lying out in the open. And, if they tried to keep it in the kitchen, the smell would give them away. There was silence for a moment when Lila suggested that they hide the tray in Cecil's bedroom. Cecil anted up the idea by adding that her closest is the perfect place. Gwen closed the cracked door and held her breath as both women walked slowly past her door. Within a few minutes, Gwen heard a knock on her door.

"*Gwen. Gwen?*" It was Cecil.

"Yes, granny?"

"Gwen, your mommy and I have to go out today. I'll be back later today and she'll be back, hopefully, in a few hours. You're in charge. I don't want to see any of my grandchildren going past the house so they can stay inside and watch T.V.

"Yes, granny!"

Gwen waited a few minutes after she heard Cecil and Lila close the front door and walk down the front steps before she left her room. She walked out of the front door and stood in the middle of the road, looking up the hill to make certain that the taxi was nowhere in sight. She walked in Cecil's room and searched all of Cecil's known hiding spots: under the bed, in between the mattress and box spring. She also peeked in the half shut door of her closet but she didn't see or smell anything. She was frustrated and was really hoping to be eating her grandmother's famous chocolate and pecan cookies.

***

Everyone loved Cecil's cookies. Now Cecil would never admit it, but she knew her cookies were something to be desired... so much so, she always kept the ingredients to the cookies to herself. Some thought she put in vanilla and coconut oils. Others thought she put in Irish butter cream with splash of rum. Still others swore that they tasted apple with a twist of lemon and grape juice. In the end, it didn't really matter because Cecil was vague even with Lila. One time, Lila made a duplicate batch of cookies by imitating Cecil's every move. But no one ate Lila's cookies especially when Cecil's was available.

***

Gwen walked in and out of Cecil's room throughout the morning annoyed. She knew she heard Cecil say something about cookies, hide and room. Gwen prided herself on stealth. Stealth was the language that Gwen spoke frequently. In between orchestrating, giving her younger brothers and sisters their baths, she would re-visit Cecil's room, convinced that the cookies were being held hostage and it was her duty to liberate them.

Gwen decided to look under the bed again and now checking to see if the cookies were hidden in the coils of the box spring when she heard,

"Gwen...Gwen! What are you doing there?"

A voice by the doorway called. It was her younger brother, Phillip. He stood there with a towel wrapped around him and soap suds falling down the side of this face. Gwen noticed a puddle forming on the ground beneath him.

"Nothing, now get back in the bathroom and wash that soap out of your hair!"

"Gwen, what are you doing under Granny's bed?" Phillip persisted.

"Nothing, I'm looking for my slippers, now get out of here!" Gwen screamed.

Phillip turned around and walked to the bathroom. Gwen quickly walked to the door sidestepping the puddle and slammed the bedroom door. It was then that she heard the rattling in Cecil's closet.

At first, Gwen was going to ignore the rumbling and let Granny fix whatever fell. But she thought, what if Cecil heard that Gwen was in her room and something was out of place. How would she explain both issues? It wasn't worth the risk to be lazy, so she walked over to the closet.

She opened the door wider and knelt down to fix the shoes when she saw cookies scattered all over the Cecil's church shoes. Gwen looked up and saw a plate teetering on a small ledge in the dark, hidden corner of the closet.

Without thinking, Gwen reached up and grabbed a few cookies and stood up cramming them into her mouth. She tried to both savor the taste and to eat as fast as she could.

She arranged the remaining cookies on the plate and put it back on the ledge. *Would Granny remember how many she made? Was it two-dozen or twenty? Eighteen?* Gwen wagered that Granny would remember. She re-folded the tin foil and set her mind that it wasn't an issue.

The taste of the cookies drew her back again and again. Each time, Gwen would tell her siblings that she needed to go to the bathroom while they were in the front of the house playing. The twenty cookies became eighteen. Eighteen became fifteen. Fifteen became a dozen. And it was taking the last bite that Gwen found herself looking at Phillip who was standing in the doorway. He was staring inquisitively and intensely. In shock, knowing she got caught, Gwen tried to think fast on what she should do. So she balled her fist and rested them on her waist.

"Well! What are you looking at?"

"*What are you eating, Gwen?*" Phillip said softly and slowly.

"Nothing!" Gwen quickly replied.

The boy walked over and reached up to wipe the spec of gooey specs off Gwen's mouth.

"*Oooh, you have cookies!*"

Not waiting for him to finish,

"I'm not eating cookies, I'm eating rice and beans."

Phillip's eyes lit up.

"*Gwen, I want a cookie. Can I have a cookie, please? Please Gwen, please Gwen?*"

"No, I'm not eating a cookie. This is left over from last night. Do you want me to warm up some rice for you?"

Phillip rubbed the piece of chocolate between two of his fingers and smelled it.

"*But, this smells like chocolate.*"

"It's not chocolate. Didn't you hear what I just said? It's the beans that are with the rice. I don't have any cookies."

She grabbed Phillip by the shoulders and turned him around and pushing him out of Cecil's room in the direction of the front door.

"*Gwen, I want a cookie!*"

"I don't have any," Gwen said but now noticing Phillips shirt.

The shirt had a dirt stains all over it and there were several tears in the shirt.

"What happened to your shirt?"

Phillip looked up to Gwen,

"Robert pushed me down and I fell over this pipe and scraped my knees and I ripped my shirt."

Gwen looked down and his blood-stained knees and the scabs that were now developing. She looked at Phillip,

"Take off that shirt and go wash your face and take this rag and wipe your knees."

When he went to the bathroom, Gwen went to check on the cookies. At first, she was settled to just make certain that the cookies were where Cecil had left them. But, she couldn't close the door before she heard the cookies calling her name, yelling for attention.

The dozen was reduced to seven. The seven down to five.
Now Gwen had a stomachache. She folded the tin foil on the flat plate. She was now able to stretch the foil's edges over the entire bottom area of the plate. But something didn't look right, Gwen wondered. She taped the top of the plate and the big, mountainous bulge was now a flat plane. All of the remaining cookies had their own space on the plate. They could even slide freely without bumping into each other.

'Oh, my gosh!' Gwen thought to herself. 'I'm going to get a whoopin!' She leaned over to the window that was facing the front of the house and noticed that the sun was going down. She knew that either Cecil or Lila would be returning home soon.

She paced around Cecil's room. Many thoughts came to her head. Everything from a strange man breaking into the house and running into Cecil's room, to running away and joining the army. Nothing made sense. Then she thought, if things got crazy, she'd could run up on the roof and jump off. Lila and especially Cecil wouldn't risk the embarrassment of having a child hurt herself over some insignificant issue like cookies.

'That's it!' Gwen smiled to herself. 'They'll forgive me because they'll think I'm crazy and depressed.' It was not the best idea but she'd reach for it if nothing else came to mind.

She remembered the five cookies and thought about her younger brother catching her with the cookie in her mouth. She knew that Phillip wasn't fully convinced, so she thought what would happen if Phillip found the cookies and Lila and Cecil caught him?

***

Gwen walked into the bathroom and picked up his torn shirt and walked back into Cecil's room. She took the shirt and rubbed the chocolate smudges from her mouth on to the clean part of his shirt. She then balled the shirt up and threw it on the ground.

Then Gwen walked to Cecil's closet and took a cookie and broke it in half. Crumbling the pieces in her hand, she sprinkled some crumbs on the floor, leaving a trail that went from Cecil's closet to the bathroom. She went to her room and got a piece of peppermint candy that Mr. Charlie had given her. She walked from the room and put the candy on the table and the half a cookie on a nearby chair.

When her plan was completed, she walked out of the house and as she sat down on the steps, she noticed the image of a taxi coming down the hill toward them. She knew it was Cecil and Lila, she knew Cecil's hat silhouette anywhere.

Gwen called Phillip over and hugged him.

"I'm sorry for yelling at you. Do you forgive me?"
"Yes."
"Okay, I left some candy for you in the kitchen."
"Thank you, Gwen. You're my favorite sister." Phillip said as he raced up the stairs and into the house.

The taxi pulled up and a moment later, Cecil and Lila came out. Cecil looked at Gwen, who was sitting on the step.

"How was everything today?"
"Okay." said, Gwen.

Looking at the rest of the children in front of the house except for Phillip,

"Did you give them a bath?" Lila asked Gwen. "By the way, where is Phillip?"

A moment later, Phillip came out of the house smiling with chocolate smeared all over his face while holding the peppermint candy in his free hand. Cecil was frozen for a second. Then, she adjusted her glasses,

"Boy, what's that on your face?"
"A cookie, granny!" Phillip said smiling and showing the gap in his top front teeth.
"A Cookie! Where did you get that cookie?" Cecil said solemnly.
"I found it on a chair in the kitchen." Phillip said proudly.
"You found my chocolate chip cookies, didn't you?" Cecil said in a lower voice, hurrying into the house.

Lila glared at Gwen,

"Didn't you mind these kids?"

"Yes, momma. I've been with them all day, here. He's been the only one whose been going in and out of the house. He keeps having to go the bathroom." Gwen said.

Phillip was quiet but perplexed by what was being said. He felt he was getting into trouble but didn't know why.

"But momma, I didn't do anything."
"You went into your grandmother's room, didn't you?" Lila said.
"No momma, I was playing out here all day."

Gwen spoke up,

"That's a lie. I saw you in Granny's room earlier today and I asked you what did you want."

At that very moment, Cecil was heard screaming.

"Lord Jesus, these kids ate all of my cookies! Lord Jesus, help me!'

Lila grabbed Phillip by the ear and led him upstairs and into the house, but not before turning to Gwen,

"You, too. Come on inside."

Phillip protested and cried that he didn't steal anything and he wasn't lying. Gwen just stood there, folded her arms and looked at him with disappointment. Lila walked back and forth from Cecil's room to console her as she knelt down on the floor by her bed praying. She walked back to the living room,

"Gwendolyn Faye, how could you let this happen?"
"But, momma, I've got all those kids to watch. How am I supposed to follow him around and watch the others outside?" Gwen said

apprehensively.

Lila looked at Gwen for a second trying to read her expression. She turned to Phillip what are you doing playing in your clean school shirt?

"I put this on because Robert tore my play shirt"

Lila put her hand out.

"Let me see how bad it is. And, take off that shirt right now. I'm not doing laundry but once a week. You kids think money grows on trees."

Phillip returned with the crumbled shirt in his hand and handed it back to Lila. Lila unraveled it and as she inspected the huge dirt stains, the tears and then she looked at the brown stains at the bottom of the front of the shirt. She leaned in and smelled it.

"What is this?" Lila said as she slapped Phillip on the side of his head.

Shrugging his shoulders, Phillip said,

"I don't know."

"You don't know, huh? Lila said as she put her clinched fists on her waist. "Oh, so you think I'm stupid. What did I tell you about going into my bedroom room or your grandmother's room?"

"But, momma," Phillips said pleading. "I don't know, I found the cookie on a chair...right there, ask Gwen?"

Lila inspected the shirt.

"Gwen, do you know anything about this? Don't lie to me, girl."

Gwen looked at Phillip for a second before she made eye contact,

"Momma, I don't know anything about cookies. I told him that I didn't have any cookies, I sent him inside to get a candy that I saved just for him. That's it."

Lila looked at Gwen for a moment and looked at Phillip.

"Come with me," she said to Phillip as she was pulling him into another room.

As she walked by a big belt was laid across the old chair in the living room.

"Gwen, I had better not find out that you're involved." Lila slowly closed the door behind them.

Gwen stood there in silence as she heard the sound of the belt whistling through the air. She could hear the sound of that half-inch belt hitting the mark. A second later, Gwen would hear a new scream out of Phillip. This went on for another ten minutes.

In the other room, Cecil was heard blowing her nose and grumbling to herself. Gwen knew she had made a mess.

CHAPTER

Lila and Abram planned a small, private wedding with an exchange of vows and a few of his close friends. As usual, the neighbors had something to say. They never approved of Lila's personal choices. To them, she was a loose woman who had bastard children from various men.

Lila, although scared at the prospects of finally being married turned to Cecil as her and Abram stood before the minister. Cecil said nothing but she held her hand tightly as tears slowly ran down her cheeks. Michael and Gwen were fidgeting the whole time. Michael, in particular, had a hard time keeping his hook-on tie straight; Gwen would twirl around very fast to see her long dress open like an umbrella.

"*Sit down, you two!*" Cecil said as they caught her attention. Five minutes later they were back at the same routine. Before long, they were both slumped on the chairs sleeping right beside each other.

***

In the years that passed, the bed that Michael and Gwen shared became more crowded. Instead of sleeping beside each other, they now found themselves sandwiching their new siblings. The bed that held two, now held six. Three slept at the foot of the bed, three at the head. Every morning, without fail, Cecil would open the door to see the apples of her eyes gently sleeping.

Shortly after the last sibling was born, there was a knock at the front door. Cecil came out the kitchen and noticed Michael's paternal grandmother, Bernice Lowery. But, both called each other Miss Cecil or Miss Bernice, as was this genteel, Southern custom.

"*Good morning, Miss Cecil. My, you look beautiful this morning!*" Bernice said as she leaned in for a hug.

"Oh, Miss Bernice... I don't know what to do with my hair. I tried this shampoo that this woman at church recommended now my hair is so dry, see look here, I'm afraid if I go walking outside I might start a brush fire. Lord only knows how I haven't burned down this kitchen yet."

Bernice shook her head and walked in carrying two grocery bags.

"*Miss Cecil, it's so good to see you. I know I need to invite you over for dinner but every time I set my mind to come over, something happens and my mind just draws a blank. But, I came here this morning because I want to ask you something and I hope you don't mind me imposing on you.*"

"You're not imposing on me. My door is always open. You know that." Cecil said and both women sat down on the living room couch facing each other.

"*Listen,*" Bernice said carefully, "*I've been thinking... well, my husband and I have been thinking; by the way these are for the newborn and the other is just some things we had lying had up in the cabinets.*"

As Cecil peeked in the bags, she saw clothes for a newborn and various other sizes as well as canned foods in the other bag; she looked at Bernice put the bags to the side.

"Thank you, now, you hear. That was very thoughtful of you. We could use clothes for the baby. But, you didn't have to."

"*No!*" Interrupted Bernice, "*We wanted to. It's the least we can do, besides we'd like to ask you something...*"

At that moment, Lila walked into the living room from the back yard and just when she was about to move the bags from out her way, she made eye contact with Bernice.

"Good morning, ma'am."

"*Good morning, Lila Mae. It's so good to see you. I came by to see how you were doing and to bring you a little something.*"

"That's so thoughtful of you, but you didn't have to."

"*Now how does that sound to hear my grandson's mother be so stoic? I was just about to ask Cecil something but I'm glad you're here because it involves you, too.*"

Both Cecil and Lila suddenly found themselves at her attention.

"Where's my manners; Bernice?" Cecil said as she got up. "I just made a pot of fresh hickory coffee. Please will you have a cup with us?"

"If it would be no trouble, sure," Bernice said as she smiled at Lila.

In a few minutes, Cecil came back with a tray carrying the coffee, cups and condiments in small dishes.

"Thank you," Bernice said as she received a cup from Cecil. As all three women had cups in their hands, Bernice placed her cup on the floor next to her feet. "Lila, I'd like to ask you something and I hope you don't take this the wrong way. I only... excuse me, we only mean good by it."

Lila had a look of concern when she asked,

"What is it, Miss Lowery, is there something wrong?"

"No, no dear; nothing like that. I've been thinking... and I'm asking this for myself as well... could we have Michael to live with us? He really could help us as it's been getting harder for Mr. Lowery to do all the things that he used to do so well."

"Keep, Michael? What do you mean, Keep Michael?" Lila asked.

"Lila, we're family and we've got more room... I mean we have so much space that it would be selfish of us not to offer a room for Michael. He could spend his days here and he can sleep in his own bed at our house. That would give you a little extra room for your growing family."

Lila seemed frozen at this awkward moment,

"I think I need to think about this. This seems so sudden."

Cecil looked at Lila and placed her hand on Lila's.

"Lila Mae, I know this is a shock to you, but I think this is of God."

Lila looked at Cecil, wondering whether her biggest supporter was now betraying her.

"But Momma, I don't know if I can let my baby move out, he's still just a boy."

Cecil gripped Lila's hand a little more firmly,

"Lila Mae, it's not like he's moving away from us, he's only going to be a few feet, maybe a few yards away and he'll essentially be living with his father's parents. They're not strangers, Lila Mae. I know how you're feeling. Don't get me wrong, this is God helping us to lighten the load. He'd be coming home every day, he'll just be sleeping in another room."

Lila looked at her, looking for some recourse. She looked back at Bernice. "I think I need some time to think about this... but I guess it may be all right. Just let me sleep on it and I'll let you know." Looking back at Cecil, "Right, momma?"

Cecil nodded in agreement.

***

Despite being in separate houses, Michael saw Gwen every day. He came over to the house every day after school and stayed for several hours before it was time to go to his father's house to do his homework and chores.

Each morning with his hair neatly combed, school clothes meticulously creased and schoolbooks under arm, he still found a way to wave to his family on the way to an upscale, but segregated school. The decision to send Michael and not Gwen to the upscale school was clearly Michael's father and grandfather whom insisted on it no matter what the cost or sacrifice. Still, this made no sense to Gwen who just wanted to follow in her brother's footsteps.

***

After school was a different affair. Michael had to find where all of the neighborhood kids were. Usually, they were behind the school jumping the ditch and playing in the woods before they went home.

To the neighborhood kids, being able to jump the ditch meant you earned your honorarium into the halls of greatness. This meant you were in the big leagues that separated the men from the boys and or the boys from the girls.

All of the kids from the neighborhood learned how to jump the ditch, missing your landing meant falling into a wet pile of mud and decayed glob that stained your clothes that even several washings couldn't get out.

One occasion after being warned by Lila to not go to the woods to ditch-jump, Gwen went anyway, confident that this time she'd make the cut just like everyone else. Gwen rolled up her sleeves and started about five feet further from her last attempt, hoping that the momentum will carry her to victory. She dug her pointy-toed shoes deep into the moist ground, took a deep breath and off she went. In her mind, she saw the extra feet as the launching pad for her newly found fame. With her right foot halfway on the ground and halfway off of the edge she lunged for the other side. She saw all of her friends clapping and rooting her on, as she was weightless for all of two seconds. As she prepared to make the step on to land, she wasn't able to raise her leg to accommodate for the natural force of gravity and she stubbed her left foot against the side of the embankment. She found herself flipping into the ditch and into a world of trouble.

Michael who was some distance away watching with anticipation ran to the edge of the creek and saw his sister cover from head to toe with who-know-what that lived, died and recycled in that pond.

It was a long walk home that night, but Gwen managed to sneak inside the house and hide her clothes before Lila saw her. The next day was a different story. After Lila came in from doing her chores that Cecil gave her, Lila called her to her room.

"Gwendolyn Faye, what did I tell you about going to the woods."
"I'm sorry, momma, I won't do it again. I promise." Gwen pleaded.
"Go outside right now and find me some of that vine you just raked up from the backyard. Don't come back here without at least three of them!" Lila yelled at Gwen as she tapped Gwen over the head as she walked out of the room.

At few minutes had passed and Gwen hadn't returned.

"Gwendolyn Faye, I'm waiting for you. The long you take to get back here, the worse it's going to be."

Gwen slowly came into the house dragging two pieces of withered vine behind her.

"This is the only thing I could find, momma."
"Oh, so you take me for a fool. You don't think I know what you're up to. I know you were back there hiding those switches. Just for that you're going get a few extra for thinking I'm some fool. Now, get in there and take off all of your clothes."

"But, momma-" Gwen cried as she tried to hug her mother for mercy.
"Gwendolyn Faye, get your narrow behind in that room and do as I say."

Gwen cried as she walked in the room. As Lila got ready, she heard Gwen cry even louder.

"You can cry and scream all you want, just make sure you have your clothes off when I get there."

Lila drank a big glass of water and wrapped the two pieces of spinach vine around her hand. When she opened the door to Gwen's room, she found Gwen huddled behind a chair in the corner with nothing but her undershirt and panty on.

"Get over here, right now young lady."

Gwen pleaded her apology but knew that she disobeyed on purpose and knew the risk she was taking when her friends goaded her to jump.

Lila walked over and grabbed the chair and put it in the middle of the room. Gwen refused to get up. Lila adjusted the strap on her hand and opened the blinds and window to let more light and air in. Lila then, ignoring Gwen's pleas, pulled her up and told her to lean over the chair.

"Take off these clothes right now, young lady."

Gwen slowly removed her underclothes while pleading in vain for mercy.

"Lean over!"

With one swing the vine caught Gwen on the arm and she quickly got up and over to the chair.

For the next five to seven minutes, enduring her mother's tears and sorrow of failing to chastise her more when she was young, all Gwen could think about was the people in the neighborhood walking by seeing her bare bottom getting switched. Her friends would later tease her that they watched as the switch would almost bounce out of her mother's hand after each blow to her rear.

Michael took Gwen's situation as a watchword. Still, he longed for acceptance that would only come from shared group experiences. As they walked home one day from the woods, and after Gwen found a way to successfully jump the ditch, Gwen was consoling her big brother for him not being allowed to play with everyone else when they heard their names called. When they looked up, it was their Great-Aunt Gladys, but they simply addressed her as "Aunt Gladys."

Aunt Gladys was standing in the doorway and had just finished cleaning her house and getting her fishing poles and hooks ready for her weekend trip. When Gladys saw Michael crying, she was moved to ask why. She went to her bedroom and came back with her bag. She leaned over and looked and Michael and said,

"Can you keep a secret?
"*Yes, ma'am.*"
"Tell me what size you wear and where your grandmother is getting your school clothes from."
"*Why, Aunt Gladys*" said Michael through his tears and red eyes.
"I'm going to buy you another set of school clothes. And, I'm going to keep them here for you." Gladys said, while hiding her mischievous grin.

Gwen started smiling, as she understood where Gladys was going with this.

"Listen carefully, now Michael!" Gladys said slowly. "You can go and play with the rest of your friends but make sure you play carefully and don't get yourself hurt. But, I want you to have fun with your friends. Play, have fun, get dirty if you want, that's all apart of growing up. And, if you get your clothes soiled, you can come here get a shower and put on the clothes I have for you here and then go home. Do you like that?"

"Yes, Aunt Gladys!"

A smiling Michael said as he turned to Gwen who was also excited. For the first time in a long time, Michael didn't feel ashamed to be his age.

CHAPTER 9

This day started off like any other ordinary day until Gwen got to school. For the first time, the teacher told the class that there was going to be a school assembly. Gwen didn't know what to think, but it didn't matter, she knew she would have to follow suit like everybody else. All of the teachers for all of the grades and all of the students who attended the school went to the school's gymnasium. The teachers stood in front of their class while the students sat on the benches behind them. A few moments later, the principal and vice principal came out and walked into the middle of the floor. It was obvious from the tears coming down the vice principal's face that it was not going to be good.

The principal began to address the teachers and the students with a warm greeting followed by very important information. They told them that the state of Kentucky was going to close their school at the end of the year and there will be other school closings in the area as well. This would mean that everyone would have to be reassigned to another school in the upcoming months.

When the principal was done talking, he dismissed everyone to go back to class. Gwen's teacher recapped and explained to the students in more detail what that actually meant. Once done, the teacher handed out a form that each child had to take home, have signed by their parents and returned by the end of the week.

When Gwen got home from school she immediately told her mother and grandmother. When asked how she felt about it, Gwen looked at Cecil and Lila and told them she was excited. It was a trying moment for Cecil and Lila because it meant that if Gwen were to transfer to an all-white school she may be subjected to a kind of personal and brutal racism that she only heard about from a distance. It weighed on their mind for the next few moments while Gwen dropped her book bag and walked outside to play with her friend.

The next morning, Cecil was is the kitchen making breakfast for the kids before she went to work for Miss Barbara. Lila was about to go to prepare the bath for the smaller kids when she thought about Gwen and the changes it would have on her. She turned around and walked out the front door and watched as Gwen and three of the girls from the neighborhood, Oletha, Mary and Jacqueline walked together out of her sight.

Her attention was frozen for a moment after the girls had walked out of eye view. Lila slowly turned around to get Gwen's little sister ready. She picked her up to bathe and wash her hair as she began to think about a situation that happened a few months back when she asked Gwen to accompany her to Krogers to get some grocery and some items for Cecil to take to work.

***

Gwen was outside playing with Oletha while Lila was ready to leave. Lila told Oletha that she could come, but only with her mother's permission. They walked some distance to run a side errand before they took a taxi to the supermarket. Along the way, a man and two boys came walking out of the bushes holding some Ring-Neck pheasants. Gwen and Oletha squirmed as they noticed the necks of the birds flopped over the fist of the men.

The boys, noticing the girl's reactions, began to make obscene gestures toward them. One of them even using expletives, "Niggas what you lookin' at? Go home niggas before we shoot you, too. The last one directed at Lila. Lila had just turned to motion the girls not to stare but to keep walking when she made eye contact with the men. The older man stood right there and smiled as his precious offspring continued to spew vulgar obscenities to the women.

Oletha took one step forward and raised her middle finger. Gwen was about to do the same but Lila knew Gwen would also have some choice words of her own to return. Just before Gwen made a move, Lila grabbed her by the arm,

"Gwendolyn Faye! Gwendolyn Faye. Stop. Don't say anything."
"But, momma-" Gwen protested.
"Listen to what I'm saying; don't say anything. Let's get going; I have to get back because I have a lot to do when I get home."

Then Lila tapped Oletha on the shoulder,

"Oletha, ignore them. They're ignorant."

Lila pulled Oletha in front of her and looked at Gwen at the same time.

"I want you two to listen to me. These people are never going to change. They will always be ignorant people. We may not have much, but we're better than them. We don't have to stoop to their level. I want you to honor the sacrifice that we've made for you by not being like them."

Then Lila pointed into the direction of the bush the men came from. "You see that Gwen? You see that Oletha? That's where they come from, the bush. They're uncivilized people. You see this road we're on? We are the future. You are our future. This road will continue. I want you to be able to see what is beyond it. They're ignorant. They're stuck in the past. It makes no sense arguing with fools like them. You hear me?"

"Yes, momma." and *"Yes, Miss Lila Mae"* were heard in unison.

"Let's go girls, we're running late."

***

That memory stayed with Lila for the rest of the day. Even as she washed her youngest daughter's hair, she wondered about her future and what will the world be like when she's a woman. At that moment, Cecil knocked on the bathroom door.

"Child, did you hear about the picnic and baseball game tomorrow over by the park?"

"No, momma. I don't know if I can go. I have to finish sewing some clothes for Mr. Benard and do some hems for Mr. Casey. I've just got a lot of work I've got to finish before church on Sunday."

"Alright, now but you promised those kids they can go. You can't go back on that promise." Cecil reminded Lila.

"Momma, can you go for me? I have to finish my work." Lila looked down and noticed she had allowed soap to get into her daughter's eyes, "I'm sorry, baby."

"Okay, I'll go but I had promised Sister Ethlyn that I would help her rehearse her solo with her at church tomorrow. But, she'll understand."

At school, Gwen was sitting talking with Mary at her lunch table when a boy walked by and brushed her feet with his sneaker. As she looked to see who it was, she recognized that he was James Campbell. She leaned down and picked up a small piece of paper that was hidden from Mary's view.

"People can be so rude, don't you think?" Gwen said as Mary looked around to see the back of Campbell disappear around the corner.

"I think he's ugly and he never says anything to anyone." said Mary said with annoyed.

"Yeah, he's a square. Okay, I'm going go to the bathroom before class. I'll see you there, okay?" Gwen said as she pulled up from the table.

As Gwen left Mary to finish her lunch, she casually went in the same direction that Campbell did. As soon as she turned the corner, she unfolded the note and it read: *"Meet me at the spot tonight at 6:30"* Gwen crumpled up the paper and as she walked toward class another boy stopped right in front of her.

"When am I going to see you?"

It was Dwight Davis, and he, like James Campbell lived in Gwen's neighborhood; they were next-door neighbors. Gwen tried to move around him,

"I don't know. I've got to babysit tonight."

Dwight moved in front of her again.

"When you gonna' make time for me? You forgot the good time you had last week?"

"Dwight, move, I gotta' to go to class. You only talk to me when you want something. Move, let me go." Gwen moved around him,

"Maybe Sunday night over at the spot."
"Alright, Sunday. I better see you there."

Dwight smiled and cocked his head they way he did when he had his way; even his teachers thought of him as cocky.

***

The evening came. Michael had to go home to do chores before tomorrow morning's baseball game at the park. Cecil hadn't come home yet from work and Lila had just laid down on the couch after making lunch for the kid's afternoon picnic. Gwen came out of the bathroom freshly bathed and was wearing a fragrance that she normally doesn't wear when not going some place important.

As she carefully walked into the living room, trying hard not to wake Lila, a creek in the floor gave Gwen away: Lila opened her eyes.

"Where are you going, Gwendolyn?"
"No where, momma. I was... I didn't wanna' wake you and ask if I could go to Aunt Glady's"

"Aunt Gladys at this time?" Lila said still half a sleep.

"Aunt Gladys had promised to show me how to make those biscuits. I'll promise I'll be back in about an hour or so. So, can I go?"

Lila turned her and muffled,

"Get back here right after. I want you here by 8, I don't want you walking the streets alone at night."

She noticed that the clock in the kitchen said 6:15. With that, Gwen walked out of the house briskly. She hurried down the street and raced through the field to "the spot" that she and James created.

James stood by a long, old divided tree. Some say this tree had a fight with itself when it was born because half of it wanted to grow east the other wanted to grow westward. He looked at his watch and it said 6:45.

"You're late. What took you so long?"
"I couldn't leave my house until just now. I'm here, so are we... "

Gwen said almost looking for some resistance.

James walked over to her and they looked around as to see if anyone had followed her into the woods this time.

"I like your perfume. Who bought it for you?"

Before he waited for his answer, he knelt down below her and put his hands up her dress.

"I got it as a gift, my Aunt didn't... like the... the ahh... it anymore."

Things were getting a bit tense at that moment. She felt her panty slide down her legs and lay at her ankles. James helped her get out of one leg but let it sit on the other so that if they were caught, no one would find the evidence laying on the ground. James stuck to his routine just like Dwight had his. It was different on very few occasions, where she'd have to start. But yet in the end, Gwen never got what she was hoping for: to be someone girlfriend.

She made it back home before the curfew and pulled out a notebook from the bottom of her clothes draw. In it, she marked down another count with an asterisk next to a capital J. It was her way of keeping track of who got what and when.

***

This Saturday morning was one the family would never forget. It started off the same as any other. None of the kids wanted to get up, yet Gwen found herself shivering because one of her younger brothers peed the bed and she was in the freezing wet spot. Gwen got up and went to the bathroom to get cleaned up. With all that was going on, a scent drifted into the bathroom from outside that distracted Gwen from thinking about the baseball game today. It was the smell of fried bacon. Gwen looked toward the window and visualized strips of bacon popping in a skillet. The red meaty center and white flabby sides turning magically to a caramelized brown and silver grey color. It was all too much for her to deny.

Within a couple of minutes, she was cleaned and wearing her favorite blue jean shorts, flowered shirt and white canvas sneakers, so she raced out the house on her way to Aunt Gladys's.

When she got there, Gladys was in the front room watching Gorgeous George take on the Bruiser. Gwen always marveled at Gladys fascination with wresting. What was it about these guys who cheat in the ring and always win? Why doesn't the referee see the foreign objects that the bad guys hide in their trunks? It was so frustrating. Gladys was too occupied to say hello to Gwen personally, instead she just waved in between someone getting thrown out of the ring.

Gwen also knew the routine. She walked slowly into the kitchen and right where she'd expect it to be, there was a plate that had fatback bacon strips, cream style corn and a country biscuit. Ordinarily, she'd wait to be offered something to eat, but it seems as if every Saturday was the same thing: Aunt Gladys in varying stages of getting ready to go fishing would run back and forth from the bedroom to the living-room to watch wrestling. There it was, a clean kitchen with the exception of this one lonesome plate. Gladys never said anything about the delicious plate of food, so this became Gwen's de facto Saturday morning breakfast. And, she was just fine with that.

After she waved goodbye to Aunt Gladys, she wanted something sweet and thought about Mr. Charlie. She wrestled with the idea of stopping at Mr. Charlie and going straight home but decided that she could spare five minutes.

As she walked to the back of Mr. Charlie's, making certain to duck beneath the side windows so that his wife, Mrs. Hassett, wouldn't see her, she came across a scene she'd never forget. A girl in the neighborhood, not much younger than she, was standing on the top step of the backdoor facing Mr. Charlie, who was in the doorway. She stood there with her hand out and palm facing up. She was holding a handful of candy but Mr. Charlie's left hand was forcibly holding her arm up. As he held up one of her arms, Mr. Charlie's other hand, his right hand, was up underneath her dress moving back and forth. She was holding pieces of candy and looking away while Mr. Charlie smiled and whispered something to her, but Gwen was too far away to hear what was being said. The girls made eye contact and the horror on her face scared Gwen. Both the girl and Gwen stood there frozen, with every muscle in the body immobilized. But in that moment, looking at her friend, Gwen felt the pain of Mr. Charlie's hand in her own pants.

Gwen walked backwards very carefully for she remembered Mr. Charlie was hard-of-hearing. Once she was away from his house she ran home and went right to her room. She was scared to tell anyone what she saw.

A few hours had passed, yet Gwen still felt as dirty as if she were pulling herself out of the ditch that she fell in. She wrestled whether she should tell Lila but Lila was running in and out of the house finishing the jobs she was commissioned to do. She thought about her grandmother Cecil, but she looked at how frail and thin she had become and worried that such news would not be good for her health.

Thoughts continued to race in her mind. 'Maybe I can tell Aunt Gladys', she thought. 'But how do I tell her? Would Aunt Gladys believe me? How could I prove that her next-door neighbor was doing that to a little girl down the street?' Gwen couldn't believe that nobody had ever seen or heard those things about him? What if she were the only one accusing Mr. Charlie, how could she face him again? What about the candy she got from him?

She decided that she'd wait and she how she felt later. Perhaps she'd get a chance to break it to Nanna, during a break at the baseball game.

***

The area's park was adjacent to the middle school and in front of the woods where all of the neighborhood kids had their clandestine meetings. It wasn't very far from Cecil's house either. The word had spread fairly quickly about the community picnic, barbecue and baseball game and everyone was looking forward in being there.

Cecil had Gwen help her with the younger children. This meant, in addition to bringing the lunch that Cecil had prepared the days before, Gwen had to bring a bag with extra towels, wipes and baby bottles.

"Uhhhhh... do we need to take all this stuff, granny?"

But, Cecil paid Gwen's question no mind. It wasn't too long before they were ready to go.

Once they arrived Cecil insisted that they find a spot near the shade. Cecil had on one of her old, broad brimmed hats that she no longer found fashionable to wear to church, but she knew it would be just perfect for sunny, humid days like this. One of Gwen's younger brothers brought the jugs of water. It took him 15 minutes later to catch up with everyone, as it was a bit heavy for him.

It was now after 2 pm and everyone who wanted to come was there. Everyone had made their way over to all of the "older folks", as they were referred to, and offered their greetings. Cecil sat on a small fold out chair and before long; she was joined by other seniors whom she'd see in church or in passing in the nearby area.

***

The neighborhood where Cecil and her family lived had changed over the years. People whom built their houses alongside Cecil had either passed away or moved closer to their children or grandchildren who lived elsewhere and the houses became the residences for younger, middle-aged families. Many of whom, Cecil knew casually by face, and very few she remembered by name. But, it didn't matter; to them Cecil was this nice, elderly and godly woman who worked all the time to take care of her family; even when she didn't have any help.

***

A couple of hours had passed and Cecil was not the wiser for it. She was in the midst of lengthy conversation that veered from God, to President Eisenhower, a handsome senator from Massachusetts to family recipes, and from crocheting to grandchildren.

'It is a beautiful day', Cecil thought to herself. As she looked around she saw some of her neighbors that she hadn't seen in a long time. She realized it took a softball game to get them to fellowship together so, she made a mental note that she would make a concerted effort to visit her neighbors more often.

She was watching the boys who were playing the field just a few feet away. She looked at the pitcher, then she looked at the catcher and the kid on the infield and wondered, 'Are these the little boys who walk past my house during the week?' She also thought of her own grandkids. 'What will they become when they're of age. Where will they go? Will they want to stay here in Madisonville?'

She had a lot of thoughts about the children, her grandchildren and their friends, as she looked at all of her grandchildren sitting next to her in the stands. She was cautiously optimistic. As the people around focused on the game, she began to as well.

The batter was up but he was behind the count *1 and 2*. The pitcher threw a fastball. The batter hit the ball as hard as he could to run as fast as he could to first base. Almost immediately as he began to take off for first, his bat flew out of his hands and through the air. Everyone saw it coming and moved out of the way as this projectile headed straight for audience. They were all able to dodge it, but little Sharon, who was only 3 years old, was unaware of the game and didn't see the bat as it headed directly towards her. The head of the bat landed and fiercely hit baby Sharon in the temple of her head. She immediately fell limp and hit the ground. The people around watched as this horror story played out in real time before them. It all happened so fast; even reaction couldn't catch up with reality. The screams from the people around demanded attention from the action of the game.

  Fear and shock instantly took over Cecil, but in a moments time allowed adrenaline to instantly take over. Cecil picked up her bleeding, wounded and dying granddaughter and ran into an epic rage. With the all of the strength and might she could muster, Cecil ran with Sharon in her arms while screaming at the top of her lungs for someone to call the ambulance and send for help.

CHAPTER

6:15 p.m.
8:37 p.m.
11:03 p.m.
1:45 a.m.
3:20 a.m.
4:35 a.m.

It was all touch and go throughout the night but the lead surgeon was hesitant about expecting too much, too soon and especially for a full recovery.

It was all just a blur to Cecil. It all seemed unreal. Sharon, her youngest grandchild, her baby, at only three years old, now with a bandage around her entire head and blood soaking through all of the layers: it horrified and repulsed her at the same time.

She was a woman of faith; she had to remind herself of that. How would it look, she thought to herself, if she couldn't keep it together in the midst of a crisis? This is that is exactly what I prescribe to those who come to me looking for comfort.

She glanced back up at the clock above the doorway and it was just about 5:10 a.m. She had to get ready to clean a house at 7:30 sharp and two others after that, but she wouldn't leave her granddaughter even if Lila didn't show up. She sat down again, this time she recognized that her heart was racing very fast and she felt lightheaded. A nurse stuck her head in the door and asked if she needed anything to which Cecil replied,

" A cup of water, please."

The nurse came back and gave her a cup of water. When she handed her the cup, the nurse's hand gently brushed against Cecil's and she noticed that Cecil's hand was abnormally hot. Cecil tried to downplay it but the nurse put on her stethoscope and placed the instrument to Cecil's heart. She gently reached for her wrist and stared away as to not make eye contact with Cecil.

"You're very hot and your heart rate feels abnormal. When was the last time you had a check up?"

"Nurse, it's been a while, I've been so busy and now look at what happened to my grandbaby."

"I understand Mrs. Oldham but you have to take care of yourself first. Can I schedule you for an exam with our physician?"

"No, no that won't be necessary. All I need is some rest and I'll be fine. But, thank you anyway. I'm just waiting on my daughter to get here because I have to be someplace in a little more than an hour from now."

The nurse stood there looking at her for a second. She felt that the pulse rate was alarming but under the circumstances, she couldn't force Cecil to get examined. She turned around but before she walked out of the room, she turned back around to Cecil and wanted to say something but seemed refrained. As she left Cecil's sight, Lila walked in. Her eyes were bloodshot red and she sobbed in Cecil's arms.

"It's going to be all right, dear. Don't you worry, the Lord has everything in his hands. Don't fret about anything. It's going to be all right. The Lord is the same, yesterday, today and... and...."

Lila raised her head and said, *"Forever."*

***

Cecil finished her shifts with all three clients, even finishing them early enough to get a half hour catnap in before the next bus came. Cecil was back at the hospital at 5:45, just early enough for her to run into the doctor before he left for the day. He draped his lap-coat over his arms as he was walking past her toward the exit when he stopped, turned around and said,

"Mrs. Oldham...Mrs. Oldham, excuse me for a second. *I know I haven't given you a lot to ease your mind, but you have to know that I had to be resistant from telling you what you wanted to hear and not as I see the situation."*

Cecil stood there in silence.

"But," the doctor interjected, "*I have some promising-- I'm not saying, good-- I'm just saying promising news.*"

Cecil smiled and started walking faster to him.

"Please tell me that there's a chance she going to make it"

"*All I can say is that her vital stat's have dramatically improved from just 18 hours ago. I can't say this for sure, but if her condition continues to improve at this rate, you may see up to... hear me now, up to full recovery, but with physical and mental therapy for... for at least some time in the foreseeable future. By the way, the nurse also told me this morning that she checked your heart rate and blood pressure and she's very concerned. And, so am I. At your earliest convenience, please make an appointment to see me. It's for your own good.*"

"Thank you, doctor. I promise, I'm coming to see you soon. Bye for now."

"Goodbye, Mrs. Oldham."

***

Cecil had been doing double shifts and missing choir practice in lieu of more time at the hospital with Sharon. When asked by the hospital when was the mother expected, Cecil would always answer with "Soon, we're taking shifts." But only she didn't notice how the fatigue was really showing itself. Cecil wouldn't take time off to sleep at home, she didn't want to be away from Sharon any moment she didn't have to. However, one afternoon while at the hospital, Cecil couldn't get up to go to the restroom without help from the staff. She called the nurse for assistance to help her get there. Cecil noticed that her legs had trouble moving. They felt unusually stiff and heavy, like she was dragging an extra hundred pounds. There wasn't a bathroom in Sharon's room, so she had to go out into the lobby and use the main restroom there.

When she left the bathroom, she walked very close to the wall and leaned on anything in that path. She would walk a little; then stop. Walk a little more; then stop again. When she had no more strength to move her leg, she just simply stood there and caught her breath. When She got back to the waiting area and sat down, she noticed that her legs were swollen especially the left side. She knew she couldn't do this one more day so she had one of the nurses to call a taxi for her. When he arrived, she asked the nurse to go into her purse to pay the driver ahead of time for her.

Cecil was barely strong enough to raise her arm to wave goodbye to the nurse. She waited to make sure Cecil was okay as she drove off in the taxi. They both knew that Cecil would have done better had the circumstances been much different.

About 20 minutes later, the taxi pulled up in front of the house and Cecil thanked him in a very soft, almost unperceivable volume. She reached for the wooden railing and took one careful step up at a time until she was able to negotiate the top landing without extra trouble.

***

Morning, afternoon and evening had passed and Cecil laid asleep. It was unusual for this amount of time to pass without Cecil getting up and doing some kind of chore, or even while she was simply waiting for the pot to boil for coffee.

Lila pulled up a chair in front of her and watched her for hours, sometimes stroking her hair or fixing the sheet. When she finally got up, she went to the hospital to see Sharon. But before she left, she would tell Gwen that she was in charge and to make sure that if she were to return late, to put the night light on outside and to make sure everyone was to be in bed. No exception. Gwen, on the other hand, had to stay in the room with Cecil and keep a close watch on her.

Lila held her big daughter.

"I'm so, so proud of you. I promise that I'll make it up to you." She hugged her daughter and said, "I don't want you to stay up to late. If you feel sleepy, you can lay down next to her."

Lila stayed at the hospital all night. She hadn't planned to but feelings of guilt hounded her. As she closed her eyes, she could hear her thoughts screaming at her. How could she have not been there to watch her children? Why didn't someone grab her daughter and bring her back to momma? What if she had brain damage? What kind of life will she have? What will people think of me if my daughter dies? Lila was haunted by the thought of what would happen even an hour from then. She felt a bit more relieved when she saw the clock nearing a new hour. It meant that they had survived another hour and the past hour meant her body was still recuperating.

Lila opened her eyes and looked at Sharon sleeping peacefully in her hospital bed. Although this time, the drain tube attached to her head was not filled as high as on previous days. Things must be getting better, she deduced as she made a judgment about how much less fluid was in the container. The guarded feeling of hope disappeared quickly when she saw the clock strike, 6 a.m.

She, with a quick, gentle hug and coat draped over her arm, raced out of the hospital and grabbed an empty taxi that had just dropped off a patient. Lila was home in 20 minutes and quickly walked up the stairs to an unlocked front door.

"Who is it?" a groggy Gwen said from Cecil's bedroom.

"It's momma, dear. I'm back. Is everything all right?"

Lila said as she took off her shoes so the sleeping children wouldn't be awoken by the sound of hard-heels on the wooden floor. Lila crept into the room to see Gwen slouched over hugging Cecil who was still asleep.

"Gwen...Gwen" Lila said in a low voice while softly tugging at her shoulders. "Gwen, I'm going to make breakfast see if you can help me feed her when I come back with the oatmeal"

"Yes, momma."

Lila walked out of the room and into the kitchen. Gwen could hear the sound of the pots and pans rustling and the big container of water that Michael fetched for them last night, being pushed on the floor. Then Gwen turned her attention to Cecil whom she heard faint groans from.

"Granny... Granny, you have to get up, Momma's making breakfast."

From the side she saw Cecil's eyes open, her mouth was moving but no sound was coming out. Gwen sat on the edge of the bed looking at Cecil. As she looked at Cecil's sullen eyes, she turned away not wanting to see what was clearly obvious. She touched Cecil's shoulder and moved her arm down, slowly caressing her seemingly lifeless hand. Gwen turned Cecil's hand over and clasped it the way she used to when she was a young girl. In a moment, she looked at Cecil's bare fingernails.

Gwen smiled and remembered hearing her grandmother telling her mother, while rushing off to work one morning, the reason why she didn't wear makeup and fingernail polish had nothing to do with religious rules and everything to do with practicality...

"I don't have the time like you do," Cecil said to Lila who was still wearing her nightgown. "I've got to work so we can have food on the table and a roof over our head. Looking pretty and all of that is your job. That's the story of your life, not mine. You sleep; that's what you're good at. You invented the term beauty sleep, not me."

***

Gwen smiled as she looked at Cecil again. She fought the thought of her grandmother, her best friend and the person who took her on cleaning trips with her not being around. She gently stroked Cecil's hair back into place. Her thoughts went back to a moment that Cecil told her; something she had never told to Lila.

***

"Granny, how do you know when you're in love?"

Gwen said as she walked up to Cecil as she prepared breakfast at the home of a client. Cecil stopped for a second and took the long wooden spoon out of the oatmeal and laid it on a wet napkin to the side.

"Girl, you're too young to ask about such things. You should be thinking about your school work and your choir rehearsals not.."

Cecil stopped herself from going any further as she realized that Gwen's honest question didn't deserve a scolding.

"Okay, what I'm about to tell you is just between the two of us, do you hear me?"

"Yes, granny," a smiling Gwen said.

"Alright," Cecil said, "when I was about your age, I had such a crush on a boy in my class. And, I did everything I could not to have those feelings for him. But nature is what nature is.

In those days, you had just one classroom and your teacher taught you all of your subjects. And, we had assigned seats. You just couldn't sit where you wanted to. That was a no-no. "Although, I tried to ignore him, somehow we always saw each other. I'd see him at lunchtime looking at me. I find pieces of paper in my notebook asking me, how was I doing? But, he left no name on the notes. One time, he was daring, telling me that I looked really pretty that day." Cecil chuckled, "I never knew how he got those pieces of paper in my notebook."

"Well," Gwen looked at Cecil, "what else?"

"Now, now. Take it easy. One day at lunchtime, I walked out with my friends and sat down by a tree and everyone took out their lunches and desserts from our brown paper bags. I looked around and saw him with his friends looking at me. I pretended not to notice him but I'd occasionally look at him from the corner of my eyes.

Without saying anything, he and his friends got up from the table and walked toward us. We stopped talking and just looked at them. They came and stood in front of us without saying anything, then each of them sat down beside us.

He opened his lunch-bag and took out his sandwich. His friends did the same thing. He leaned over and gave me half of his sandwich. I looked around and saw his friends do the exact same thing to my friends. When I seen my friends accept the sandwiches, I turned to him and took the sandwich.

Me and my friends ended up giving them our desserts and he was my first everything."

***

Gwen quickly readjusted herself on the bed to sit Cecil up. It now became apparent that something was wrong with Cecil.

Lila had just got a fire underneath the pot when she heard Gwen screaming for her. She cut off the stove and ran to the room. When she got to the doorway, she saw Gwen cradling Cecil's head in her chest while saliva oozed from the right side of her face, the left side looked frozen.

"Gwen, go next door and call for an ambulance! Go child"!

Lila got on the bed and looked at Cecil. Cecil could move her eyes and her right hand slightly but she was totally immobile on her left side. She even felt cold to Lila on that side.

"Momma, everything's going to be all right! Momma, I promise you, everything's going to be all right. Momma, I'm gonna' get a good job and you won't have to work anymore. You can stay home and crochet, you can go fishing with Aunt Gladys, you can sleep in all day if you want to, whatever you want, whatever you want, just whatever you want to do, Momma!"

Lila looked down to Cecil and saw her eyes closed,

"Momma... Momma..." Lila shook her head, "Momma! Don't leave me! Don't leave me..."

Cecil barely opened her eyes but when she did, Lila knew she was leaving.

Tears streamed down Lila's face as she held Cecil. It felt as if time had stopped and the worse possible thing was happening right there and then and she was powerless to do anything about it.

"Momma, I can't go on without you... Momma, I need you... Your grandkids need you... Momma, I can't... I can't..."

Just then she felt a slight movement by Cecil's hand. Lila grabbed her hand and looked at her. Cecil was able to straighten out a finger and slight movement of her arm. Lila leaned over and snatched a pencil that was on the nightstand. She looked around but didn't see anything to write on and didn't want to let go of Cecil's hand. She reached across the bed and picked up her bible. She opened to the back of the book to a blank page and put it underneath the hand that was holding the pencil. Lila slipped the pencil into Cecil's hand in hopes that maybe she could write something down. It took Cecil a while but when she let the pencil slip from her finger, the message read:

"Can't?"

Lila looked at Cecil trying to figure out what that meant, but, again, a response couldn't be mouthed. Cecil touched the pencil and with crocodile size tears in her eyes, Lila looked at the pencil and put it in her hand again. Cecil wrote, this time:

"Can't never could and never will. Never give up on God." The pencil dropped from her hand again.

Aunt Gladys was on her way over to bring some food for the family. She had bowls and dishes full of food weighing in her arms to take to the kitchen, but that quickly fell to her feet outside when she heard the sounds of Lila screaming and the children crying hysterically.

***

The funeral was 10 days later. It seemed like a scene right out of the movie, "An Imitation of Life." What should have been a 3-hour service went on for almost six.

The normal church congregation itself was about 100 members, but on this day there were close to 750 people in attendance. There had to be two services to accommodate all the people. The Pastor himself seemed occasionally surprised and bewildered by the number and the racial makeup of those who came to pay their respects.

In addition to the families in the surrounding neighborhoods around Cecil's house, you also had people from different communities who had never ventured in this area before and never would again. Lila, most of all, was surprised by all of the well-wishers and platitudes bestowed on Cecil: most, if not all of the stories of Cecil's generosity and benevolence were received far beyond Lila's ability to grasp it in that painful moment. Yet, she was getting a sense of the life that her mother lived and did anonymously. All of her children were there except for Sharon, who was scheduled to be released in a few days, but under a doctor's supervision

When the second services had finished almost 11 p.m. that night a program from the service drifted around and fell, then got tumbled around the doorway of the church. With the front side up and many footprint stains, the inscription underneath the photo read:

"We will miss you as much as Heaven is happy to see you."

CHAPTER 11

   Early one morning, as the window curtain rose and fell with each passing gust of wind, a gentle melody awakened Gwen. It wasn't loud enough for any of her brothers and sisters to hear it, but the sound gently nudged her awake. She leaned up and strategically knelt into those spaces between arms and legs to get out of bed. Her nightgown was wet from her youngest brother's offering but the sound of this song took priority at that moment.

   She walked to the window and stuck her head out hoping to see where this sound was coming from. She closed her eyes too, but she only knew it was coming from somewhere out of view. She walked to the bathroom to change and get ready for school. Since Cecil had passed away a few months before, she promised Lila and her great-aunt Gladys that she'd help even more with the siblings. But today was the first day at the new school and she was both terrified and excited at the same time. As she was washing the soap off her face, she couldn't and didn't let that melody to leave her mind.

***

Gwen decided early on that she wanted to try something different. She had always heard that the "white schools" had air conditioning, cushioned seats, an hour long lunch period in a cafeteria where lunch was brought to you on a waiter with metal forks and knives. She also heard they had olympic size swimming pools and paddle board courts. She thought to herself, she could do those things although she was terrified of water.

When Gwen approached Seminary Junior High School, a lady with horn-rimmed glasses and a long plaid dress that fell about calf length, greeted her at the entrance of the school. She extended her hand to Gwen and said her name as if in a confirming tone.

"Gwe... Gwendolyn Faye... Collins?"
"Yes, ma'am." Gwen said very softly.
"Welcome. Come right this way."

The lady whose name Gwen forgot ask for walked very briskly up the pavement into two double wooden doors. Gwen marveled at the ornate woodcarvings over the doors; it was a far cry from her last school.

Gwen clutched her bag and pressed her notebook against her chest. As she walked behind this long, slender woman with black lace up heels, she looked around and noticed pockets of kids looking at her and whispering. Her instinct was to say hello but the looks on their faces warned her against it.

They walked to the guidance counselor's office and Gwen waited almost fifteen minutes before she was told what to do next. They had given her some handouts to give to her teachers to sign and return by the end of the day.

Throughout the day and even at lunchtime, no one sat or even spoke to Gwen once. She heard grumblings but nothing that she could make out. The only pleasant experience she had was with her math teacher, Jerry Sisk. From the moment she walked in the door, he gave her a warm yet loud welcome. While the class was working on an assignment, he walked through the rows and stooped by her desk,

"I want you to know something, Gwendolyn, I'm here for you. Any problems, any questions you may have I am right here. Don't worry about anything, you're going to have lots of friends here. It is our honor to welcome you to our school. You are one of us, now."

The sentiment caught Gwen by surprise. All she could say was,

"Thank you, Mr. Sisk."

She left school that first day with the lasting memory of his kinds words playing in her head. It wasn't a bad thing that she thought he was very cute as well.

Gwen met up with her friends on the way home. They decided they were going to celebrate the first day of school with a nickel dip of ice cream from Ted's Restaurant.

"Where is Michael?" Oletha asked.

"I don't know. When I saw him this morning, he asked me where'd I be after school. I told him I'd be with you guys. He said he had something important to tell me." Gwen said in response.

"Did you hear that new song from Otis Redding? They were playing it at the Paradigm." Mary said excitedly.

"Wanna' stop by when we're finished?"

"Girl, I got a lot of homework. They about to nearly kill me with all this reading I've got to do tonight." Mary said. "Besides, I want to know what happened to your step-father. No one's seen him and you haven't said a word about him."

Now, both of her friends were looking at her. Gwen took a deep breath.

"Abram's in jail."

Both Mary and Oletha looked at each other in shock.

"I don't know what happened. Momma came home real late one night and she told me I needed to help her to keep this a secret from my younger brothers and sisters because their his and momma's children together."

"Well, what happened?" Mary said.

"I don't know everything, but momma said that Abram came home from work early and told her that he needed to pick something up from the supermarket and he left. She thought it was some groceries or maybe something that he wanted her to make for him for lunch tomorrow. Anyway, she said, Miss Linney came over and told her that she had a telephone call. Momma said it was the police and that she needed to get down to the station as soon as possible, they arrested Abram for stealing a woman's purse in the supermarket's parking lot."

"When did this happen?" Oletha said.

"About two months ago. Momma still couldn't get over the fact that granny had died in her arms and when this happened with Abram, she just wanted to make it go away quick. So, she told me if anyone asked where Abram was, he was in another state on business or with relatives and that he'd be back soon." Gwen said, as she ate the last piece of cone.

At that same moment, the girls heard a whistling of a bicycle headed toward them. It was Michael and he was smiling.

"I thought you'd be over by the ditch."
Gwen looked up,
"No, we just wanted come here to get some ice cream."
"Wanna see what I made?" Michael said as he looked around at Gwen and her friends.
"What is it now?" Oletha said with a twinge of sarcasm.
"I just opened up a school in the smokehouse! Isn't that great!" Michael was beaming from ear to ear. He was so excited he forgot to ask Gwen how was her first day at school, something that concerned him from the very beginning.
"Wanna see it?"
"I don't know," Mary said hoping that something more urgent would come up immediately so she could have a reason to be elsewhere.
"Let's go! It's gonna' be fun. Wait till you see what I've done." Michael lifted up his bike and turned it around. *"Come on! I gotta" get back"*

***

No one knows how a "smokehouse" came to be but it's known to have had a long history in the Carolinas and in Mississippi.

Originally, a smokehouse was a place where hunters and/or butchers cured meat after it was captured. And, in this house a meat was cut into different sections and hung in certain areas where the butcher would prepare the meat for long or short term storage.

A smokehouse is roughly the shape and size of a two-car garage, the average being about the size of a single-car. In certain areas, Kentucky in particular, any sized detached dwelling was sometimes called a smokehouse.

In Madisonville, the best-known smokehouse was owned by the beloved Mr. Bowman.

Over time, when the need for specialized and segregated houses for meats became unnecessary or new residents moving on to a new property inherited a smokehouse with the acreage, the smokehouse would be used for other purposes such as storing coal for the winter months.

***

Michael's paternal grandmother, and the generations before her used the smokehouse that was out back for all of the above mentioned reasons. But after they went to a gas stove, the "coalhouse" as it was now referred to, became a packed, storage unit.

At the beginning of summer while Michael was raking the leaves and throwing out the garbage, he asked his grandmother if they had any use for their storage unit. She didn't have any use for it, but she would get with Michaels grandfather and see if he needed it for any reason. She told him she would let him know. Her husband didn't have a goodenough reason why she shouldn't give it to Michael. So, she called Michael aside one afternoon and made him promise to keep it clean and to put it to good use or his grandfather would repossess it.

"Granny..." Michael told her at the time. "*You're going to be very proud of me. I'm going to turn it into a classroom and I'm going to have a school just like yours.*"

"Oh, Michael, that's so wonderful."

After Michael showed Gwen and her friends the converted coal house, now a makeshift classroom, complete with six desks, six chairs and weekly readers, it would be a place that many of the neighborhood kids would go to after school and at recess.

Michael rode his bike alongside Gwen and her friends as they walked the trail from his grandmother's house to his mother's house across the field. Since they didn't go to the wooded area to jump the ditch and play an assortment of random games, they arrived at Gwen's home about an hour earlier than usual.

When they walked up the stairs they were surprised to see some neighbors that they only knew by face, sitting in the living room with Lila.

"Hi... momma..."

Said Gwen as she looked around to these strange faces. The air was filled with a cheap scent of alcohol, while dark colored bottles laid across the living-room table. As Michael walked into the house, after resting his bicycle on the front lawn, he was equally surprised at what he saw.

Lila had a bag covering a bottle by her feet, but she moved the bottle underneath the couch.

"Gwen, Michael, go inside the kitchen I made dinner early.... How was your day at school, Gwen? Did you make any friends?" Lila said as she looked in the direction of her company.

They didn't wait for Lila to introduce them so they immediately began gathering their belongings and slowly walked past Michael and Gwen without saying a word.

Gwen looked at Lila while Michael waited until the company had left before he walked out and rode home. Then Gwen walked to her room without saying a word. That was an unspoken secret between him and Gwen, that their mom was different.

CHAPTER 12

Some time had gone by since Gwen and Michael found those strangers having a drink with Lila. It was not like her to drink and she certainly didn't keep company with these neighbors on a normal basis. These were some of the same people who'd whisper and gossip about her for years and now they were frequent guest in her home. It made no sense to anyone, especially Gwen.

One Saturday morning when Gwen had gone over to get that plate of fatback bacon, biscuit and cream-style corn that Gladys inevitably left for her every weekend, Gwen did something a little different. She interrupted Gladys' Saturday morning ritual of watching wrestling to ask about the changes happening with Lila.

"Aunt Gladys... why is momma having these people over?"

Gladys got up from the couch and motioned for her to accompany her to the porch.

"Gwen, my dear, when we were growing up... listen to me, I sound like an old woman... but when we were growing up, our mother, your great grandmother Sarah was very, very strict with us. She always had an eye on us and always had people watching us and reporting back to her. So, as young women we felt like we weren't treated fairly and as a result we started to do things to see if we could get away with it."

Gwen looked confused.

"Like what?"

"Well," Gladys continued, *"well, we used to go to places and do things that we weren't supposed to. I mean, let me explain. We did all that was asked of us but if we had finished a certain thing early, we'd go somewhere and do the things that everybody else was doing until we knew it was time to be back. That was our way of taking control of our lives. We used to call each other, 'grown folk.' We could do what 'grown folks' did."*

"So, you and granny did sneaky stuff?"

"Well, we didn't call it sneaky stuff. We called it behaving like grown folks. We weren't kids in our eyes we were more like adults. That's what we thought until your grandmother got pregnant with this guy she barely knew. And, when she had Jack, she overcompensated and started being very strict with him. Over time, he wanted to get away and when he got that job with the railroad, he took it. And, that's why he moved to New York or some place up north."

Gladys looked at Gwen and knew that she needed an answer for Lila's behavior.

"Jack told me... he said, Auntie Gladys, when I get big, I'm gonna' move away, far away from here, you hear? And that's exactly what he did. When Cecil had Lila, she said she wouldn't make the same mistake she made with Jack. So, every time she'd hear Lila complain about something, she'd argue and fuss but then she'd give in and let Lila have her own way. And eventually, when Lila started noticing boys, your grandmother would give your grandfather a cup of chamomile tea and that would put him right to sleep. He would sleep right there on the porch in front of your house and boys could come over and talk with your mother. I always felt that Cecil was giving in too much but she'd always tell me, to stay out of it. So, I did. So when your mom had Michael and then when she had you, Cecil came over and apologized for not being a lot more stricter."

Gwen looked at Gladys,

"So, me and my brother are a mistake?"

Gladys quickly wiped her hands on her apron and said,

"No, child! That's not what I'm saying. I'm saying that it wasn't the right time and not with the right person. Sex is not bad, but sex with the wrong person is. If we didn't have sex, no one would be here in this world. What you're seeing with your mom right now is her trying to find herself. But, she's choosing the wrong kind of friends. All they're going to do is bring her down. But, she's stubborn like her mother."

Gwen walked home with a full stomach but still disillusioned about what was happening. She resolved that she'd have to be the mother if hers wouldn't. When she got to the front of the house, Lila was there waiting on her.

"Gwendolyn Faye, where have you been?"

"Momma, I was just at Aunt Gladys'"

"Why didn't you let me know, I needed you here. I've got to go to the store to pick up some supplies because I have someone coming over to pick up some clothes that needed altering. Get inside and give those kids a bath and I want those dishes washed before I get back. You hear me?"

"Yes, momma." Gwen said, as she walked past her in the house.

Gwen did as she was told. First getting all of her siblings undressed and ready for a bath. This meant that she had to have one of her sisters and one of her brothers to help carry the large aluminum bath pale from the back and fill it up with water. After two kids would bathe, the pale with the bath water would be dumped and refilled. This took about 45 minutes.

While everyone else was eating, Gwen washed the pots and pans and as the breakfast dishes came to her, she washed them too. "Y'all go and watch T.V. now. I need a break from you all," said Gwen as she sat down on the living room couch. She looked at the dirty ashtray and suddenly recognized the scent of alcohol. It was then she remembered to look under the couch. There she found an empty liquor bottle wrapped in a brown paper bag. She put the bag back underneath the couch and picked up the pack of cigarettes. They were almost unused. As she turned the pack around and around, it seemed as if only one cigarette was smoked. Hmmm, she thought to herself.

She took the pack of cigarettes and hid them in her back pocket. She made sure that her brothers and sisters were preoccupied. Then she walked into the bathroom and took the cigarettes out. She took one and posed with it in her mouth. She looked at herself from several different positions with the cigarette and imagined herself like one of those models in the magazine. Since no one was in the bathroom with her, she decided to secretly try one. Why not, she thought. One puff won't kill me. Besides, I see people do it all the time.

Gwen looked on the shelf and then on the floor to see if there were any matches. Nothing. She opened up the medicine cabinet and looked on the bottom shelf. Anxiously moving toothpaste and toothbrushes out of the way on the second shelf, she still saw nothing. Finally, her eyes looked up at the top shelf and in the corner, she found a pack of matches. When she opened it up, she only saw three left. She struck a match once, and nothing happened. She pulled another match and struck it harder this time, and she got it to light. She paused for a moment and looked at herself in the mirror. Taking in a deep breath and exhaling, she lit the cigarette and inhaled. She coughed violently few a few seconds, which, seemed like eternity, and when she was settled she tried it again. Again, she doubled over gasping for breath. Just then she heard the front door open. She cracked the bathroom door hoping it was just one of her siblings going outside, but it wasn't.

Gwen quickly fanned the air above her with everything in the bathroom she could find. She gargled, she brushed, she washed her hands three times before hiding the pack of cigarettes in her back pocket.

"Gwendolyn Faye. Gwendolyn Faye, where are you?" said Lila with her arms full with bags.

"I'm coming. I'm in the bathroom." Gwen sniffed her shirt but couldn't tell if it smelled like smoke. She walked out with a smile.

"Whew, boy was that a relief!"

Lila looked at her but didn't move. Then she took one step toward Gwen who stood right where she was.

"Gwendolyn Faye, come here for a second."

"Yes, momma. I can hear you."

"Gwendolyn Faye, I said come here. Come here, right now!"

Lila's voice was sharp, but not like the curling of her eyebrows.

"Yes, momma?"

"Have you been smoking? You've been smoking my cigarettes, haven't you?" Lila immediately put down the bags. *"I told you to come here."*

Gwen put her hands up.

"Momma, I'm sorry. I didn't mean to... I mean I just wanted to try one to see what it's like."

"So, you want to try my cigarettes when I'm not here. You're a grown woman now? Huh. Answer me!"

"No, momma-"

"Oh, I see. You want to know what it's like being a woman. You want to be a woman, huh?" Lila said as she had her fists resting on her waist. *"I got something for you. I'll tell you what. I've got something better in mind for you. Where are my cigarettes?"*

Gwen didn't move.

"I'm not going to ask you again. Where are my cigarettes?" Lila said as she took steps toward Gwen.

Gwen reached into her back pocket and pulled out what was left of the pack and handed it to her.

"Where are my matches?"

Gwen quickly glanced over at the couch and saw the pack of matches she left earlier when she grabbed the cigarettes. She ran to the couch and knelt down on the floor and picked them up. Then she slowly walked back over to her mom and handed it to her.

"Okay, this is what we're going to do since you think you're a woman. You're going to smoke all of these cigarettes, just like I do; every single one of them. Here, take one and light it."

"But, momma", said Gwen as she started to cry.

"*I said take one out and light it and put it in your mouth.*" Lila's voice echoed with a steely tone.

Just like in the bathroom a few minutes before, Gwen was now gasping for air as she struggled to grasp the technique for inhaling and exhaling. She pleaded in vain as Lila handed her cigarette after cigarette. After the fourth cigarette, with tears and mucous running out of Gwen's eyes and noise, Lila tapped the last four cigarettes out of the box and into her hand.

"*Here, take these,*" said Lila as she extended her hand toward her.

"No, momma please, no! I'm sorry, I'll never do it again."

"*I said take it from my hand.*" There was not a muscle that moved in Lila's face when she said it.

Gwen slowly took the cigarettes from her hand and stepped back. She didn't know what her mom was going to do next.

"*Now I want you to eat them.*"

"No, momma. No, I don't want to," said Gwen frantically.

"*I said eat them now Gwendolyn Faye, or I'll grab that switch for your bottom!*"

Gwen couldn't believe what Lila was making her do. With tears continuing to stream down her face, 'Why would she make me eat these', she thought to herself. Fear crept up on Gwen like a taxicab in New York City, quick, fast and in a hurry. Her hands, trembling and she can't seem to stop shaking. Knowing there wasn't much time to think with an outraged mother piercing her very soul; slowly but surely Gwen broke each cigarette into to small pieces and ate each piece little by little. The taste of dry leaves and paper made her cough a few times when she swallowed and the tobacco mixed with the tears that seeped in her mouth, tasted like bitter soil chunks that had been mixed with vinegar. Every swallow caused Gwen to grimace her face. These last four cigarettes seemed like forever to get done. When she was finished with the last one, Lila motioned for her to open her mouth.

"Ahhhhhh"

"*Okay,*" said Lila, "*now go to your room. Your grounded this weekend. Don't you ever let me see you smoking. If I catch you smoking again or if you come home with cigarette smoke on you, I'm going to swat your behind until you can't sit down for days.*"

CHAPTER 13

There was one thing that Cecil always believed and she often said it, "Follow your dreams."

When Cecil would occasionally take Gwen with her to clean houses, she'd always say to her,

"Gwendolyn Faye..."
"Yes, granny, I'm listening!"
"Gwendolyn Faye, I want you to promise me that whatever to do or whatever you become that you'll always follow your dreams. Dreams are like a compass that God gives us so that we can follow and have the life that He meant for us to have."

"Yes, granny."
"That's my little Gwendolyn Faye. Good girl."

"Granny."

"Yes, dear."

"I dream of becoming a singer one day. I wanna' be like Ella Fitzgerald and I want to sing on big stages and wear nice clothes and I want people to clap for me."

"Yes, dear. And, one day they will. I promise you. Just don't give up on your dreams, okay?"

"Okay, granny, I won't. I promise."

***

Gwen never forgot that conversation. The last thing she said to Cecil as she looked at her in the coffin was that she would never give up on her dreams and that she'd make her granny proud.

One day coming home from school, Gwen and her friend Mary saw a billboard posted to the wooden light pole that was advertising a jazz group coming to the Paradigm club. Mary saw the look on Gwen face as she looked at the faces on the billboard and knew that Gwen wanted to go. She did too, but Gwen was glued to the picture.

Gwen was silent for the rest of the walk home. Mary was talking but Gwen didn't hear a thing. Just before they stopped by Mary's house to say goodnight, Gwen turned to her:

"Be ready for nine sharp. I don't want to get there too late, my voice doesn't sound its best too late when it's dry."

Mary turned around,

"What!"

"Never mind, be ready for 8:30 because I'm going to need some of your makeup."

"No, I can't go. What am I going to tell my mom and dad?"
"You can tell them that you're sleeping over to my house, but we're going to church first."

Gwen walked off without waiting for a reply from Mary. But, Gwen's mind was made up, she had to sing and she had to fulfill her destiny. And, this is part of that stop.

After Cecil's death, fewer and fewer of the people who loved and respected Cecil stopped by to visit Lila and her children. Soon, a different kind of people came by. It was familiar faces mostly that Lila knew here and there. Now, they were regulars at her place and they always brought their own drinks, some for Lila as well.

Gwen knew their habits and she also learned about Lila's new habits. Gwen walked up the front of the stairs and into the house past all of these vagrants; she shook her head at them and gave Lila a glare as Lila stared forward hiding a glass under the couch she sat on.

Lila's guests would stay for uncomfortably long hours before someone from that group would stumble out of the house. The others would follow that lead and Lila would be left passed out on the couch until morning.

Gwen felt like there were many things that were changing, especially her mom. Ever since her grandmother died, Gwen's behavior started to get more radical, just like her mom's.

The evening arrives and it is time to head out to see the jazz band. Gwen knew she wouldn't make it out the front door without getting caught, so she had to think about how to sneak away. She looked in her closet and didn't find anything to wear to a show. So Gwen sneaks in her mom's room and peeks in her closet. She pushes away some church clothes and see's some cute dresses. She grabs the first cute one she saw and slipped it off the hanger. She dashes back to her room and tries it on. 'It fits perfectly' she thought. This will surely do for tonight. She climbed through her bedroom window wearing Lila's dress, and headed out for the road. Gwen looked at this as a great career move and a positive life experience.

Gwen and Mary arrived at the Paradigm at around 9:45. At first she was questioned, but Gwen told the security officer that she was there as guest of that jazz band and her assistant Mary, was there as a guest of the band too. It was easy to pretend you're not 13-years old when you have the body of an 18 year old.

The club was crowded and became even more crowded after 11 pm. Gwen and Mary stayed in the back of the club but would occasionally sit on a bar stool up front throughout the night. As the night went on, Gwen had caught the eye of the lead singer of the jazz band. It was exciting as well as intimidating to be the object of the band's leader. Over the course of the night, Gwen found herself singing with the group and every so often in chorus.

Near the end of the night roughly about 3 a.m., the band took a break and walked over to the bar. The bandleader politely walked behind Gwen who was still awestruck from his attention.

"Hi," he said as he gazed into Gwen's eyes. *"Do you work here or are you with another group?"*

"No... I live here in town and I decided to come here after work to unwind and have some fun," said Gwen.

"Well, I just want you to know that I had fun too, especially watching a pretty lady such as yourself having a good time."

"Why thank you."

Gwen said trying to hide her nervousness.

"*Are you a trained singer because you're really good out there? The band and I heard you singing all night in the crowd.*"

The singer motioned for another drink then he pointed to the waiter to include a drink for Gwen.

"*I'm sorry, I forgot my manners. My name is Dean and whom do I have the pleasure of speaking with?*"

Gwen struggling not to loose her composure,

"My name is Gwendolyn Faye, but my friends at work call me, 'Gwen' for short."

"*That's such a beautiful name,*" Dean said.

Now measuring Gwen up from head to toe.

"*Say, if you'd like, would you like to come with us and sing with the group. You really do have a nice voice and I think it will compliment the group to have a fresh face and a new idea.*"

"I don't know what to say?" Gwen said.

"*Say, 'Yes' and it's a done-deal. We'll take care of the rest.*"

"When would I start and how much would I get paid?" Gwen said inquiringly.

"*That all depends on how big the venue is. The bigger the venue, the bigger the pay. Say, let me ask you this. We're headed out of town tonight. We have a gig up in... in... I forgot the name but my band member, Bosely, will tell you if you want to find out. But, you should come with us. This could be a good break for you and for us.*"

"I...I... don't know what to say. I need a minute."

Gwen said as she turned looking for Mary. Mary was there a moment ago or was that an hour ago.

"It seems as if you're friend is gone." Dean said somewhat mockingly. "Now you have no one to keep you back."

Gwen said nothing to his comment but thought about the possibility of going on the road as a lead singer. She had gotten here so far without anyone's help or support, why should she be concerned about what others think of her. She sat there for a few moments and turned to Dean:

"Okay, but I don't have any clothes to wear."

Gwen remarked.

"Don't worry about a thing," Dean said confidently, "We can always find something somewhere. I'll buy you whatever your little heart desires. Our bus will be ready in about 30 minutes. I promise it'll be priceless."

Gwen smiled to Dean and said,

"I'm in!"

As Gwen went to the restroom to clean up, a guy playing bass openly stated that he had trouble believing Gwen was eighteen or anything near that. He pleaded with Dean to reconsider bringing a stranger on the bus.

Town after town, gig after gig, Gwen couldn't remember where she was. For the next three days, Gwen was the female lead of this band. It was everything she ever hoped for. A day of shopping with Dean came to a screeching halt when one of the band members broke the news that his new girlfriend was barely 13 years old.

Gwen could no longer lie about her age and told Dean the truth. There was an emergency meeting with all of the band members and they drove Gwen to the nearest Greyhound station and paid for her ticket back to Madisonville.

Gwen arrived later on that same evening. Looking at the sky, she wagered that Lila would be asleep, Gwen slowly walked up the stairs to find Lila sitting in the dark living room.

"Good evening, Mamma"

Lila said nothing. She just stared out of the living room window. Gwen went into her room and came back out to go to the kitchen, when she heard Lila's voice.

"Eat where you ate last night.... and while you're at it, sleep where you slept last night."

Gwen said nothing but went outside and sat on the front steps. The next few weeks would not be the easiest.

CHAPTER 14

"Hello... Hi... can I sit down and have lunch with you?"

Gwen had been resting her clasped hands on the lunch table in deep thought. It took her a moment before she even realized that there was someone standing over her and talking to her.

"Hi, can I sit next you."

The voice was from a tall, slim, lanky blond girl. Gwen had seen her before and always noticed that she was by herself. None of the other girls ever spoke with her.

"Sure. Go right ahead. My name is Gwen."

"I know. I've seen you around. My name is Lunell, but you can call me, 'Lue,' if you want."

Lunell put her tray down and smiled as she arranged her lunch to eat.

"Would you like my apple sauce? I already had one this morning and I'm getting sick of eating baby food."

Gwen smiled and happily accepted it.

The two girls talked through lunch and in between classes, ignoring the voices of those who didn't like the *colored* girl or as some would scream out from a distance, the "nigger."

One day, as Gwen and Lunell were leaving school, Lunell asked if she'd like to come to her house for a visit. Gwen looked at her for a minute because she had never been invited to a white girl's house before, much less been inside one, But they had been spending so much time together, she thought 'Why not', so she shrugged her shoulders and said "Okay!"

It was like the scene out of movie Gwen thought to herself. She had never seen a house like this much less a neighborhood with houses that were two to three times the size of her own. Lunell and her brother, a star basketball player for Seminary Junior High, lived in a huge house. When they reached the door, Lunell's mother smiled and warmly welcomed her in. To Gwen, it was like she stepped into another world, maybe even a different country. All Gwen knew was she was in the presence of a very remarkable family.

When the girls went to Lunell's room, they began talking about a lot of things that they had in common. First, they each wanted to know who was their favorite Beatle. Gwen told Lunell that she had a crush on Paul and Lunell said she fancied Ringo. Then Lunell asked why wasn't she at school more often. Gwen looked at Lunell and tried to offer something to appease her curiosity.

"I have to help my mother with my younger brothers and sisters."

"Oh," Lunell said sheepishly. *"You have a lot of brothers and sisters?"*

"I have five, but my older brother, Michael lives with his other grandmother."

Lunell tried to make sense of the dynamics but didn't want to intrude.

"Can't your parents hire a nanny to help raise them? That's what my mom and dad did."

"Their dad... their dad... died. He died a few months ago and that's why I sometimes had to stay home because my mom had to work to make money for us."

***

Just before the picnic incident and her grandmother, Cecil's passing, Gwen and her friends would go on bus rides to neighboring towns like Providence and Earlington as day trips. On each of those occasions, Gwen, Oletha, Jacqueline and Mary would always meet boys at the movie theater or at a shopping center.

And before they left for the trip back to Madisonville, they'd always exchange phone numbers. Meeting these new people gave the girls, especially Gwen, a newfound confidence in themselves. All of the girls saw themselves, not as freshly minted teenagers at thirteen but women who knew how to handle men and relationships. The girls started playing this game, a game they had fun doing. It was a game to see which guy was going to fall down on his knees begging her to marry him. They all pinky bet each other to see who'd get the most expensive gifts from the guys they met.

Gwen was the most daring. She figured that if she saw her guy more than her friends did with their guys, then she'd end up with the guy who'd fall in love with her first. But the calls to her became less frequent, Gwen became concerned and volunteered to go to see them.

This presented a number of challenges like where would she get the money and how would she avoid being seen taking a bus and not going to school. But, she'd play hooky from school if it meant she could spend the day with James in Providence or "Totsy" in Earlington, then so be it.

Sometimes, Gwen would miss a whole week of school at a time. It was worth it if she wanted a man, she told herself, as she paid the fare and got on the bus.

***

The next day at school started off like any other day.
Gwen would meet Lue by a big tree to the side of the school. Sometimes, Lue would arrive first and sometimes Gwen. Both Gwen and Lue would endure taunts by fellow classmates, but never for too long anymore as most of their classmates had other things to talk about.

But this time, after they said their goodbye's to go to their respective classes, a group of girls who never spoke to Gwen began following her in the hallway and on the staircase.

"Nigger! Nigger, you hear me calling you! Go home, nigger! We don't want you here! Go back to the Rosenwald Projects! Go home, nigger! Go home to your mammy in Carver Court!"

It startled Gwen a little bit although she was used to getting teased. Gwen turned around once to say something, but instead, grabbed her books and kept walking to class. In class, Gwen took out a piece of gum that Lue gave her when they met before school earlier. When she got to her desk, feeling upset and unsettled, she slid down in her seat a little and rested the back of her head on the top of the chair and began to chew on that gum real slow. Boiling on the inside, that gum seemed to relax her.

During class, Gwen just kept quiet, to herself, and never volunteering to answer any questions. But for some reason, she often found herself being asked to answer questions despite a wave of hands that went up. She looked around and recognized one of the girls from that group that was shouting obscenities toward her; she was sitting toward the front. The girl stared at her a moment then gave Gwen the finger.

Gwen continued to ignore but lowered her head so she'd find cover from the kid sitting in front of her. All of a sudden, the girl who taunted her raised her hand.

"Yes, Sally Mae, do you have a question?" The teacher said, surprised.

"Miss M., the colored girl is chewing gum in class. Isn't that against *the rules?"*

Miss M. stood up from her chair and looked in the direction of Gwen.

"Gendolyne Faye Collins, please stand up and open your mouth."

Gwen looked at all of the faces looking at her and she slowly got up. She opened her mouth revealing a glob of soggy chewing gum.

"Come up here, right now, Gwendolyn Faye." Miss M, sternly said.

Gwen went up in front of the class and stood before Miss M. Extending her hand palm up to Gwen's mouth.

"Give the gum, right now, young lady."

Gwen was hesitant.

"I said, give me the gum right now or I will send you to the principal's office."

Gwen was about to reach up and take the gum from her mouth, when she spontaneously decided to spit it out. And spit she did. When Miss M. looked at her hand and there in the midst was a syrupy, yellowish phlegm with the stick of gum Gwen had in her mouth.

Before the teacher could scream, the recess bell rang. Miss M. jumped back and flicked the smelly, gooey gum in the waste pail. As the kids were filing out of the door, Miss M. looked at Gwen and said,

"Young lady, you go right now to the principal's office. I will deal with you there."

And, with that Miss M grabbed a handkerchief from her desk draw and feverishly started wiping her hand.

On her way to the principal's office the same group of girls who kept taunting her, one of them confronted Gwen. She pushed her as she walked down the stairs. Out of instant reaction and reflexes, Gwen caught her balance and with her free hand, grabbed the girl who pushed her and flung her head first down the stairs. One of the girls screamed for the security officer that had just walked to the top of the stairs. Gwen jumped to the bottom of the steps for part two of the beating this girl was now about to get. With Gwen's fist balled up and with a left hook in motion, the security officer ran down the stairs and grabbed her hand and pulled Gwen off the girl. She was immediately escorted to the principal's office where Ms. M was waiting for her.

Miss M. walked Gwen to Mrs. Dean's office, the principal, and closed the door after Gwen walked in. She signaled to Mrs. Dean that she needed to be back for her next class and would check back later for Gwen's punishment.

"You know, Gwendolyn Faye, I could suspend you over the chewing gum incident and the fighting incident." Mrs. Dean said as she lowered her reading glasses. *"But, I want to talk to you about another matter, a lot more serious."*

"They hit me first. I didn't say anything to them." Gwen said in protest.

"I'm not talking about that. I'm well aware that there have been some comments said to you in error, but let's move past that to deal with the matter at hand. We know... I know... that you haven't been coming to school regularly. I have a report that you've been 15 days absent last month and 6 the month before in addition to tardy almost 12 times since the semester began. This is inexcusable."

Gwen looked down at her fidgeting hands.

"Do you know what this means, Gwendolyn Faye?" Mrs. Dean asked.

"No."

"It means that you're suspended for the next 10 days and we'll have to have a parent-teacher conference before we can accept you back. I've taken the liberty to reach out to your father and mother but I haven't gotten a response to the letter that was sent. We will send word when we're available to meet with either of your parents. I

expect, Gwendolyn Faye, that when you return, there will be no more disciplinary problems from you. Do you understand me?"

"Yes, Mrs. Dean" said, Gwen who was now grinding her fingernail in her notebook.

"That'll be all. And, your suspension begins immediately. There's no need to return to class. Please close the door behind you."

CHAPTER

Gwen was horrified. She also felt like a failure because she wanted to prove that she could make it in a "white school." She didn't want to go home early in case her mother was home from any one of her jobs. So, she decided to go window-shopping.

As she walked passed stores, she heard music coming from around the corner. She noticed that it sounded very familiar. As she put thought to where she may have heard it before, she realized it was the same song that woke her up on the first day of school. She looked up and it was coming from Kroger's grocery store.

Gwen and her friends always loved Kroger's but never had enough money to buy anything from them. It was only when she went with her mother or grandmother that she was able to get anything.

She walked around the store looking at clothes, jewelry and snacks before she realized that she needed to get home. Walking through the crowds to the exit, she notices a red, portable record player. Many of her friends had one of these. Lila had one in her room too, but they were never allowed to touch it or her records for that matter. If any of her Mahalia Jackson, Ella Fitzgerald or even Muddy Waters records were moved out of place, someone was going to be held responsible.

She walked to the display and moved her hand across the outer cover, the lock latch and even the fine stitching. She pictured this in her room playing the new 45's by The Jackson 5, Aretha Franklin, The Everly Brothers many of whom played at the Paradigm from time to time.

She lifted up the display model. It wasn't too heavy. In fact, when the top is closed, she could just get it to hold under her arm. She had held stacks of books that were just about as broad, she thought. The image of her room appeared before her. She saw the perfect space and it was high enough where her younger brothers and sisters couldn't reach it. This was perfect. So, she knelt down and tied her shoes laces grabbed her books and the red record player and politely walked out of Kroger's.

***

Lila arrived home early from work, and she had it in her mind to get inside and take a little nap before everyone got home. It sounded nice, but her reality was she didn't have time for a nap. She needed to get started on dinner early because she had some errands to finish run.

Lila picked up the mail on the way inside. As she thumbed through to see what bills needed to be paid, she saw a letter from Gwen's school.

She pulled it out of the pile and dropped the rest of the mail on the end table by the couch. She opens up the letter to read the letter as she slowly sits down on the couch.

> Dear Mrs. Oldham,
>
> We are writing to inform you that Gwendolyn Faye Collins has been suspended for truancy and she would not be allowed to attend classes until after a parent-teacher conference with the school's principal was completed. Please make the necessary arrangements to come to the school...

After Lila finished reading the entire letter, she placed it on the couch next to her. She couldn't believe what she just read, suspended? She thought to herself, 'What did she do?' Lila took a big deep breath and sighed as she laid down the couch sideways with her legs tucked into her stomach and her head resting on a pillow. While feelings of frustration began to flood her mind, She thought, 'What would mama do if she was here? Mama would know what to say right now. She would know how to handle this situation.' Feeling frustrated and too tired to think anymore, Lila slowly dozes off to sleep to escape the thoughts.

The rapid knocks on the door caused Lila to pop up out of her deep sleep. Slightly disoriented, she looks around and realizes that she dozed off. She looked at the clock and it said 3:48, she didn't expect to sleep for three hours. Seeing the letter pressed under her hand, she knew that it was real and she was not having a nightmare about that.

The knocks kept coming,

> "Lila, Lila, are you home? You have a phone call, it sounds

important and it's urgent. Lila, you in there?"

"Coming Mrs Linney, I will be there in a second.

Mrs. Linney received an urgent call for Lila, but unlike the last time, when Abram was the reason for the discretion... this call was different. There was no way Lila saw this coming. She wouldn't imagine a reason for the Police calling her, so Gwen being arrested left no such concern to be considered.

Lila walked in a fast pace to Mrs. Linney's house. Mrs. Linney was back in the kitchen washing the dishes. When Lila picked up the phone, the voice on the other end said,

"Mrs. Oldham, This is Officer Banks. I have a Gwendolyn Faye here in my custody for stealing at Krogers. Would you please come down to the county precinct right away."

Lila in shocked, dropped the phone. Anger and frustration instantly overwhelm Lila. She slowly raised her hands to cover her mouth in shock. Her eyes slowly turn and look at Mrs. Linney washing the dishes and she burst out and yells,

"Mrs. Linney, Gwen is in jail. She's in jail. She got picked up for stealing"

Mrs. Linney didn't know what to say as shock and surprise caught her off guard. She dropped the dishes that she was washing in her hands, on the floor. The impact of the dishes hitting the floor snapped Mrs. Linney out of her surprise.

"Oh shoot! What Lila? Wait, Why?

Mrs Linney began to ask these questions as to come to clear understanding of the situation, while she began to pick the broken pieces of plate fragments off the floor.

Tears began to fill Lila's face and the feelings of frustration and inadequacies as a parent began to fill her thoughts. But as quickly as those thoughts came, they quickly went. She didn't have time to think too long about it as she had to wipe her tears, and get herself together before she went down to the precinct. Lila saw the broken dishes, and began to help Mrs. Linney pick up a couple of pieces.

She clearly saw that Lila was terribly upset, and saw the phone still dangling from the chord, so she picked up the phone to see if anyone was still on the other end.

"Hello?"

"Yes, will you be able to come down to the precinct and pick up Gwendolyn?"

"Oh yes, yes sir, right away. She'll be there."

Lila stood up, fixed her shirt, wiped her face, thanked Mrs. Linney and walked out.

***

Gwen was charged with petty theft. But, since she was still a minor, she was to be released in her mother's care. Lila didn't say a word to Gwen. Lila was still upset about the letter from the school she had just received about Gwen's suspension.

When the judge was given the record and read the charges, he turned to Gwen and asked if it were true. Gwen, in tears, nodded. Then the judge looked to Lila.

"Is there anything, Mrs..... Mrs. Oldham you like to say for the court to consider?"

The judge made no secret of his disappointment with Lila and Gwen. Lila waited just a minute, hoping to say something that would rationally explain the dynamics.

"Your honor. I've tried my best... I've done everything that I know to do. It hasn't been easy on any of us. Last month, she ran away and I didn't see her for several days. I came to find out she was traveling with a band and when they found out she was under-aged, they sent her home. Now, I get this letter telling me she's been suspended for skipping school. I.. I don't know what to do-"

"I do!" The judge said as he slammed his hand down on the bench. *"I most certainly do. You, young lady, I'm going to send to reform school for a year or maybe more depending on your behavior."*

Gwen looked with horror at the judge and then to Lila. This couldn't be happening. Wait, she thought, there has to be another way.

"First thing tomorrow morning, my officers will pick you up and we'll have transportation to take you to the Kentucky Village Reform School and I hope you learn your lesson young lady, because the next step will be a prison sentence."

There was silence on the way home. Lila sat on one side of the cab and Gwen sat on the other. Each kept their hands to themselves. Privately, Gwen resented the fact that Lila told the judge, she didn't know what more to do. It was the nail in the coffin as far as Gwen was concerned because she didn't know where Lexington was or how to get to Madisonville if she had to leave.

***

It took a couple of weeks before Gwen finally accepted the fact that she was in reform school.

She was assigned to a unit managed by a woman named, Mammie Gwinn. Mammie Gwinn was about 5'7", wide like a linebacker who never smiled. She looked like the type of woman you just didn't cross the wrong way. But there was something stirring in the bottom of Gwen's stomach ever since she met Mammie Gwinn.

***

It wasn't just her appearance that scared Gwen, her big bulging eyes or invisible eyebrows. This short, rotund woman struck fear even in the company of the big, muscular security guards that were twice her height. It was something nefarious.

While getting acclimated to the new school, she sat beside a group of girls whom she recognized as living near her compound. She ate quickly and listened intently, wanting to see who was liked and who wasn't. Today, the topic on the girls' mind was Mammie Gwinn. After a few expressed opinions about Mammie Gwinn's hygiene, one of the girls screamed out that she was nothing but a big, fat, nasty.

Carlita, the quietest of the girls who sat there, leaned over the table and told the other girls not to talk so loud because Mammie Gwinn has eyes and ears everywhere. She then told them that she heard about another group of girls who'd sit by themselves in the area farthest from the lunch tables outside. They'd always had a rambunctious lunch period, but they were too distant for anyone, especially Mammie Gwinn to hear what they were saying. Security guards would have to blow their whistles for them to know recess was over.

Carlita continued, one day Mammie Gwinn hid behind a nearby tree that was blocking their view of her. After the girls made it up to this mound, they immediately started in on their daily critique of Gwinn. One girl commented that Gwinn was looking like a turtle she saw walking into the city sewer. It had eyes shaped like a frog with an odd shaped head, green teeth and a butt big enough to eclipse the sun. Another girl said that Gwinn looked like a mangy dog that just escaped from a kennel. Still, another disagreed and said Gwinn's had an upturned nose that reminded her of a pig's head in a butcher shop. And, she was certain that Gwinn used that nose to sniff out discarded chicken bones in back alleys.

After that last remark, Gwinn jumped from behind the tree in her navy blue military fatigues with an array of medals and pins that would make any army general jealous. With one hand, she held a big brown bully baton pointing at the group and with the other hand held a whistle, which was now giving off a sound that could have been heard for miles.

Security guards, Carlita said, came running from all directions. All of the girls had to lie down on the grass with the hands behind their back. With all of the guards surrounding this small group of girls, Mammie Gwinn started to tap her open palm with the head of the baton and she paced back and forth around the girls. Carlita said, one girl yelled out,

"But Mammie Gwinn, we hadn't done anything."
"So, you hadn't done anything.,"

Mammie Gwinn said mockingly.

*"So, that means that you **were** up to something. You just confessed that among other things that you were plotting to overthrow my office, my staff and worse, this entire establishment. Am I right?"*

None of the girl answered.

"Let me get this straight. One of you said I looked like a tortoise... right?"

None of the girls answered

"I see. Oh, but someone else said I looked like kin to some down and out canine, not even of the clean, housebroken variety. Ah, and yes, one of you said that I get my meals from the back of alleyway and other disagreeable and unmentionable treats that are found in such places.

I just want to thank you young women for alerting me to the problems that this school has. It is noted and greatly appreciated. It's good to know that we have such fine and astute students whose mind is not on base matters but on the safety and welfare of all who come here for one reason or another.

May I ask one favor of you charming young ladies, to whom may I have the pleasure of thanking for offering such honest and descriptive platitudes? Anyone? Oh, come on now, don't be shy, I just want to thank you personally, I feel indebted to you for your investment.

Okay. I'll tell you what I'm going to do. We, and when I say 'we', I mean myself and these fine gentlemen who make up our facilities' security force, will escort you to a room nearby to my office. It's that bolted door, you've no doubt passed by and wondered what was behind it. Well, there's something very, very special behind it. And, we only open it for special occasions such as this.

Don't worry ladies, just for your convenience, we'll have some cells prepared for your afterwards so that you may rest and recuperate before returning to your cottages out here. I assure you, you'll appreciate over time what your selfless act of courage today means to *all of us."*

Some girls began to cry and to point out those who spoke against Gwinn, but all Gwinn did was to smile and to walk in front of the group as they filed out from the field and into a doorway no one knew existed.

All of the girls at the table looked around and for the first time took account of their surroundings. Gwen had often wondered why the inmates would walk in the opposite direction whenever Mammie Gwinn would turn the corner or stop talking as she strolled by them.

Gwen didn't know how true that story was that this girl told the group but she recognized that Mammie Gwinn was someone she had to be careful of and to stay off her radar. She knew she had her work cut out for her.

***

They all lived in what the Village authorities called, "Cottages." In her cottage, there were girls her age and they reminded her so much of Oletha, Jackie and Mary. In fact, her inmate cliques often argued about the same things as Gwen's friends, mainly about boys and one in particular: Terrance. But, there was one thing everyone could agree on and that was that Gwen could sing.

From a young child, Gwen would listen closely to the radio or her mother's and grandmother's records and imitate the vocals to a tee, even the inflection of certain notes that few singers were known for mastering.

It was not unusual to see the guards come to Gwen's area and ask her to sing. It always ended with an ovation and a few tears from inmates and guards who were moved. It was during this stay in reform school that Gwen decided that singing was a part of her destiny.

The guards, however, had their hands full when these young ladies argued about something because as they heard Gwen say on numerous occasions, "I tell ya, when I tell ya, when I tell ya'" that was young Kentucky lingo for Gwen's about to have the last word. Which, she often did.

Gwen's original sentence was for a year with good behavior but because Gwen had frequently got into verbal conflicts and had to go to solitary for not being quiet, her sentence was extended. No one ever officially told her how long her sentence was.

Gwen eventually met Terrance and childhood friend, Gregory. They were about two years older than her and lived in the senior cottage of the school. Gwen met them during lunch and would occasionally talk about life outside Kentucky Village. Their daring stories about crime and clubbing and wild times in their neighborhood intrigued Gwen.

Gwen and Terrance started a relationship that led to several fights back at the cottage with girls who said, he was their boyfriend. Meanwhile, Mammie Gwinn announced that the Village residents were going on a field trip.

The field trip was one of the few events that everyone always looked forward to. But, this year it was different. Terrance and Greg learned that their release would be one week before. Gwen was devastated. She was so used to seeing Terrance whenever she wanted, she couldn't imagine being there without him. Gwen pondered on the thought of not seeing him anymore and the more she thought about it, it became more and more clear to her that she had to do something about it. But what, she thought?

Gwen told Terrance that she didn't want to stay there without him. He didn't want to leave her either so he suggested that she escape and come with him to Louisville.

"How can I?" asked Gwen.

"I know a way, we just need to plan this out." Terrance told her.

A week away from the field trip and Terrance was released from the Village and sent back home. They saw each other everyday until this point; planning and scheming on how Gwen can escape so they can be together forever.

Finally, the night came for them to leave. There was a scheduled trip into town to the state fair, and the plan was for Gwen to meet Terrance there and secretly slip out before they all line up to get back on the bus. That night Gwen was nervous. She paced the fairgrounds with the rest of the girls from her cottage. Everything about that night was a blur to Gwen until it was time for them to leave. Every moment seemed like eternity.

The time had come when Mammy Gwinn called for her troop to line up for the count. Gwen could feel the perspiration dripping from her face. As planned, she went to the end of the line. She looked over her shoulder at the big white bus and felt the opportunity to escape was then, or never. Terrance had told he'd be waiting on the other side of the fence that enclosed the fairgrounds. All that was needed, he explained to her, was for her to crawl under the fence and run for the corner where he'd be waiting.

"All aboard ladies!" A guard said. Gwen knew the time had come. Her heart began to pound out of her chest like a police bust in a drug raid. She knew she had to make a move and do it fast. As she looked over and saw the fence, there really wasn't any opening for her to squeeze through except a small little spot that if she tried hard enough, she might be able to make it through. As the line of "ladies" boarded the bus, Gwen took several steps backwards toward the back of the white bus until she felt she was in the clear to run as fast as she could to the gate. She could hear Mammie counting the girls from behind the bus. She knew it was getting closer to the end, and she had to run now.

Gwen, took off. She headed out away from anyone's view to the small opening she found. She dropped to her knees and laid on her back. Gwen slipped under the fence as she slithered and turned. She felt the jagged edges of the gate snagging and ripping her dress with every move. The sharp edges would scrape along her skin as she rushed to make it through. It was painful, but she knew it was worth it. She knew she couldn't turn back now.

As she freed her leg from the gate, she heard her name called. It got louder as they began to walk around and look for her. Gwen took off, there was no time to dust the dirt and mud spots off her clothes, she just had to run as fast she could. She headed for the corner where, to her surprise, Terrance and Greg were waiting.

"Run, baby," Terrance called to Gwen as he opened the back door of his four-door. Gwen dove in, head first and the car sped off into the night with Louisville on their radar.

Fraught with fear, Gwen stayed down for several hours as Terrance and Greg drove up the turnpike. But, when it was safe, Terrance and Greg gave her the word to sit up.

Gwen began to look at herself and realize that she did it. She made it. They got away. Her clothes were torn and dirty; she lifted up her arm and began to look at the blood and scratches that went deeper than she thought. She lifted the bottom of her shirt to look at her stomach.

She saw more scrapes and newly forming bruises. She was glad it wasn't worse than that.

When she sat up, Terrance lit what she thought was a cigarette. But, it didn't smell like the Kools cigarettes she had in reform school, the scent this cigarette gave off was nothing like she had ever experienced. He inhaled and then handed it to Gwen.

"No, thank you,"
"Aw, come on, baby! Don't be a party pooper!"

She looked at him for a moment then accepted the marijuana and took a drag. The smoke entered her lungs and made her head feel funny in a good sort of way. She told them she had smoked weed before and tried to act like I knew what she was doing.

After a few more drags, Gwen was high. Nothing seemed to concern her anymore. She told Terrance and Greg it really didn't matter what happens next, where they were taking her, or where she would be staying. She was well relaxed and didn't care. Gwen rested her head on the window and watched as the lights went by as she took in each moment.

***

Prostitutes walked freely in the neighborhood while "johns" drove up and down the street without any fear of the police. People are sleeping on sidewalks and injecting themselves with needles in front of buildings; it was not where she wanted to be. After a week of staying at Terrance's sister house, Gwen felt homesick and asked him if she could leave. She was happy that he showed no objections but he explained to her that he couldn't drive her back. Although she really liked Terrance, she realized this isn't what she wanted. She knew she would have to part ways with him. That meant, she either go back home, or go back to the Village. There was no way she could get back home... so she had to bite the bullet and go back Miss Mammie. She knew this wouldn't be good and this would probably be the last she saw Terrance.

The next day, after they said their goodbyes, he walked Gwen to a corner that was easy for the police to find. Gwen sat on the curb until a familiar car with the state's emblem on the side doors showed up.

An officer exited the car while Mammie Gwinn sat in the passenger's side. She was told to stand up and put her hands on the car. He then placed her into handcuffs and put shackles on her feet before she was escorted to the back of the car.

"You know you are in big trouble, and you are going to be locked up, after you get the paddle," Mammie Gwinn told her as she stared out the window.

The hours passed in silence, but somehow it really did not matter to Gwen what would happen. She pressed her face against the window without saying a word but cried silently as to not give Mammie Gwinn the satisfaction of hearing, "You're right." She was mentally prepared to accept her fate, even if meant expulsion or corporeal punishment in front of the other girls.

As they entered the village gate and started the long drive to Gwen's cottage, she could see people peeking out the windows.

"Does everyone know I am coming back, Mammy Gwinn?"

She did not answer; rather continued to look straight ahead. The fear of what could happen to Gwen started to worry her. Looking around at the faces looking at her from every direction, Gwen began to realize that she was in more trouble than she bargained for.

The guard parked the car and then came around to open her door to unlock the handcuffs and remove the shackles from her feet.

"Go straight to the shower to be deloused and do not talk to anyone on the way," Mammy Gwinn told Gwen as she was maneuvering herself out of the car.

Gwen looked at all the faces looking back at her as she walked in the building. Their whispers followed her all the way down the hall. But she did exactly as Mammy Gwinn told her and headed straight for the showers. After the probing inspection and a shower, Gwen was brought down to Mammie Gwinn's office.

Immediately, Mammie Gwinn, saying nothing, but only pointing to a chair in the middle of the office. It was almost the same situation playing out here like it was at home with her mother Lila. She knew the chair was meant for her to drape herself over for a beating. She did so and she tried to send all of the muscular strength she could muster from every part of her body to her backside. Gwen knew, once again, that her bare bottom was the front line of the battle.

"Bend over young lady. I bet you will never do this again." 1, 2, 3, 4, 5...29,30 – the strikes of the paddle went on and on.

Gwen counted up to thirty lashes so far, but it felt more like sixty. She held back the tears but occasionally moaned as her redden bottom was paddled mercilessly for almost 20 minutes. With each hit, Gwen told herself she was getting closer to the end.

When Mammy Gwinn was finished paddling, she laid the paddle down and turned toward the door.

"Okay, young lady. It's lock up for you. And after thirty days in seclusion, you will think twice before you run again."

Mammie Gwinn walked with Gwen as she took baby steps toward her station. The sound of Mammie Gwinn's giant key ring full of keys echoed throughout the long corridors they walked. But, Gwen didn't know what was worse: the pain she'd feel when she went to the toilet or thirty days of seclusion.

The march led down a long hall toward a big steel door. Suddenly, she was terrified and started to walk slower, not wanting to be surprised at what was on the other side of that door. Mammy Gwinn opened the big steel door and what was on the other side was a single mattress in a small cell not more than 8 feet long by 5 feet wide with an 8-foot high ceiling.

"Welcome home Gwendolyn," Said Mammy Gwinn as she left Gwen in that small cell. She turned around and walked out.

The sound of that big steel door slamming shut behind her was deafening, but the sound of the keys locking her in from the outside was worse. Although Gwen had been here before, this time, it was different. That cold, gray cell that seemed no bigger than a closet was now her home for the next 30 days.

As she lay on the hard mattress, thoughts of Lila and Michael and the rest of her sibling ran through her mind. She also saw images of Aunt Gladys's fatback bacon, bun and cream style corn on a plate. Hot and steaming. Never before had she appreciated the simple life she had. She looked up at the dark ceiling with fraying, old cobwebs drifting back and forth. The smell of rotting cheese and the residue of a dead mouse came to her attention. This was no place for her, she deemed.

She didn't know when she fell asleep but she awoke to the clank of keys.

"*Dinner time! Time to eat!*" said a voice outside her door.

She wondered what time it was, since Mammy Gwinn was gone and a new security guard was standing in the doorway.

"*So, you decided to come back,*" the guard said.

"Yeah, I did, and I am glad," Gwen said.

"*While you are in seclusion, you are to stay away from the door, do not talk to the other girls and you won't get days added to your time,*" she instructed me.

"Yeah, ok, thanks."

Gwen wondered why the guard was helping her, but she didn't ask any questions. Although it was tough, she took the guards advice and she didn't talk to anyone.

CHAPTER

"One month solitary confinement. And the next time you see fit to take off on your own, there will be worse consequences. I assure you that if you don't complete your time here, you will in a federal prison cell with real criminals, not like these delinquents that you call friends. Do you hear me, Gwendolyn Faye?"

Mammie Gwinn lifted up a long skinny belt from her desk and wound it around her hand leaving about a foot and half inches of strap hanging loose. She walked slowly toward the middle of the room.

"Yes, ma'am."

"I told you the rules when you first got here. I know you forgot so I'll just remind you. I told you, stay out of trouble and don't cause any trouble and you won't get into trouble."

"I'm sorry, Mammie Gwinn, I promise I won't do it again!!"

"I'm sure you won't. Now lean over that chair and don't you move or it'll be worse."

For the next twenty minutes, Mammie Gwinn reached back, so far back that at time the tip of the belt touched the floor behind her. Her arm whipped back like a pitcher throwing a fastball. She let the belt stay on it's mark for about half a second before pulling off of Gwen for another strike.

Gwen thought to herself this was the lesser of two evils, at least she'd be able to rejoin her group, as she heard the sound of the belt twirling through the air and making a shrilling sound before feeling its impact.

Gwen cried but she held on to the seat of the chair and stared at it so she wouldn't give Mammie Gwinn the satisfaction of knowing she broke her down.

***

Gwen served almost two full years at the facility, a few months before her sixteenth birthday. She was then back home and into the loving arms of Lila in the spring of 1968.

Two weeks later, while talking with a minister in the parking lot below, Dr. Martin Luther King, Jr. was assassinated on the second floor balcony at the Lorraine Motel in Memphis, Tennessee. Gwen and her friends, Oletha, Jacqueline and Mary were standing outside talking when Michael came running down the street.

"Quick, quick go inside and change!" Michael said while panting. "Y'all go home and change into black and me back here!"

"Wait, why do you want us to change?" Gwen said.

"Just do as I said. They just killed Dr. King, so let's go over to Tucker's and sit down and eat!" Michael said insistently.

Oletha looked at Gwen and Michael,

"You want us to go to Tucker's to sit down and eat?"

"Yes, now let's go! Hurry up! We've got to do this tonight!"

Michael turned from Oletha, Jacqueline and Mary back to Gwen and pushed her to go inside.

Fifteen minutes later, they all stood in a group of four wearing all black. Michael bent down and tied his shoelaces and brushed off his shirt and pointed forward.

"When I start chanting, you chant behind me. Okay? So, let's go!"

As they went on their way to Tucker's Grocery, a segregated restaurant and supermarket. Where local African-American families and young adults would buy small groceries or items from the back door. Usually, you'd just see school-age children standing around eating their single scoop of ice cream, while around the front, white patrons were given menus as they walked in through the front doors and into the restaurant.

A single male voice followed by three female voices coming up the street was heard calling out, *"They killed our leader, but they can't kill us!"* *"They killed our leader, but they can't kill us!"* *"They killed our leader, but they can't kill us!"*

In a single file, they brazenly walked into Tucker's Grocery and sat down quietly. No one from the restaurant, nor any of the patrons said a word. There was no movement and no sound in the restaurant for several minutes, perhaps as Michael thought, a calm before the storm. No one, including Michael was certain that Tucker's management or its white patrons knew of Dr. King's death, but for him it was time to make a statement. He and his paternal grandmother had marched with Dr. King just a few months before and the right for integration was, for them, long overdue.

A short time later, a woman came from the back and politely asked Michael what would they be having. Michael looked around and answered softly. Then, Gwen and Oletha and Jacqueline and Mary.

After she took their order, she came back and spoke to Michael.

"I'm sorry for what happened to Dr. King. I truly am. But, we can't serve you here at the counter. I was told by my manager to give you the food you requested but then you'd have to leave. I'm really sorry for your loss."

The waitress returned with the food and looked at them. Michael looked at her and the other staff who were looking his way. He turned to the waitress and said,

"Thank you, very much. We'll be leaving."

Each of them was handed a container with the dessert they ordered. Then Michael looked down the row where Gwen and her friends were sittings and said.

"Let go! March!"

He nodded to the waitress when he made eye contact with her, then he faced the door and said,

"They killed our leader, but they can't kill us!"

The girls caught up on the next refrain and chanted this as they walked out of Tucker's.

"They killed our leader, but they can't kill us! They killed our leader, but they can't kill us! They killed our leader, but they can't kill us!"

Michael assembled the girls in front of Tucker's along the sideways and they paced back and forth down the shopping area street chanting,

"They killed our leader, but they can't kill us!"

Fifteen minutes of chanting turned into forty-five. Forty-five turned into ninety minutes and then two hours. Before he realized it, there was now a sea of people around Michael, Gwen, Oletha, Jacqueline and Mary chanting,

"They killed our leader, but they can't kill us!"

Someone from the local newspaper was alerted to the demonstration by the small group of teenagers and had a reporter and a photographer sent to interview them. As the reporter was speaking to Michael and asking about how Dr. King's life would impact him and local area African-American teenagers, Michael reminded the reporter that the crowd of demonstrators consisted of many different nationalities and age groups and that Dr. King's influence defied cultural and intellectual boundaries.

When the reporter asked Gwen the same question, she looked at her brother and said,

"It's just like my brother said. We are one."

Then Gwen noticed one of the demonstrators in the crowd. She was an acquaintance from grade school but she was wearing a nurse's uniform. The sight of this uniform intrigued her so she walked up to her and greeted her. The acquaintance wrote down her number on a sheet of torn paper and handed it to Gwen and then she left through the crowd.

CHAPTER

***

Gwen found the number in her pocket from her friend she saw at the march and decided to give her a call. It was a great catch up on each other's life. Gwen's friend told her that she works as a nurse through the Job Corps program and that it was a successful opportunity for her.

Gwen found a great deal of interest of what her friend was telling her and began to think of how she could enroll. She knew her mother was not going to let her go, but she had to do something to get in there. So, Gwen pleaded for weeks, perhaps even a couple of months before Lila would allow her to finish her schooling in the Job Corps program.

She was initially denied eligibility because she hadn't turned 16. But when she did, she and Lila went to the office and filled out the paperwork. Lila looked at her just before signing her name and asked,

"Are you sure you want to do this?"

Gwen smiled,

"Yes, momma! I can study nursing and maybe if they have a singing program, I can get into that as well."

With that Lila signed her consent.

***

The Job Corps program was the centerpiece of President's Johnson's, War on Poverty initiative. Started in 1964 by the Director of the Office of Economic Recovery, Sargent Shriver, the program was modeled after a similar by-then discontinued World War II era program, Civilian Conservation Corp or the CCC.

In both models, the goal was to create a new, skilled labor force by training young people between the age of 16 to 24 with free vocational and certain academic training for a period of up to four years, most being a two-year program. The program also hosted the participants with a stipend and room and board.

Gwen signed up for a two-year nursing program but after structural re-organization for the region, Gwen and four friends she met in the program opted to be re-located to Charleston, West Virginia to complete their studies.

It would be the turning point in her life.

Gwen was now settling into her new life in the Job Corps program.

She lived in the housing they had provided with a roommate and community of busy students and workers. One afternoon as Gwen walked out of the vocational training center during her lunch hour, she decided to explore the downtown area. When she turned the corner and saw people coming in and out of a restaurant-bar, she got very curious.

She stepped closed to the sidewalk to see the name on the marquis. It read, The Juke Box Bar and Restaurant. She noticed there was a lot of activity in the restaurant as she came closer to the glass front doors. 'What was happening inside which made it a popular spot', she wondered? She cracked open the door and the scent of greek food came billowing out, at the same time the iconoclastic sounds of Patti LaBelle, the Rolling Stones and Bob Dylan filled her ears.

She saw an area that looked like a stage near a jukebox. She watched as people randomly walked to that area to sing along the songs that was playing on the jukebox. Not far, leaning on a counter was an older man watching intently on those who'd come up to perform.

He kept a hand on his waist with a towel clenched in his fist while he leaned on the counter but occasionally he'd sit up take a sip from a glass next to him. He looked different than those in the restaurant but fit in as if he owned it. She didn't know what to make of it but she resolved to come back at another time to get a closer look.

She held the door slowly as it returned to its closed position and began to walk away when a voice from behind her spoke:

"I was waiting for you to come in. I wanted to buy you a drink?" said a man who wore a suit in all white.

Gwen turned around,

"Excuse me, are you talking to me?"

"Yes," he said. *"I don't see anyone else around who's breathtakingly beautiful as you. And, I don't usually talk like this to strangers."*

"Thank you!" Gwen smiled with her wide grin. "That's so nice of you. I don't know what to say."

"You don't have to say anything. Just come inside and join me for a drink. Everybody is a friend in here. Besides, it's not often when we're graced with a visit from such a beautiful woman. I'm just taken with your smile. I don't think I've ever seen a smile as beautiful as yours."

"You're making me blush and I don't even know your name."

Gwen trying to accept his compliments with modesty but outwardly she was flattered. And, she knew he knew. She didn't know what to think in this moment. Who is this man? He looks to be about 6' but anyone looks like a giant when you're 4' 10".

Gwen looked at him from head to toe. She had never seen anyone like him. Against the dirty, grey pavement was his shiny white and black, wingtip Stacy Adams in stark contrast. The wingtip was in what looked to her to be a polished, patent leather. The body had a reflective coating over the white base. The shoe strap and heel was as black as the tip but was mostly covered by the flare of his bell-bottom, bleached-white silk pants. Although he wore a black belt, white suspenders held his trousers up and only revealed themselves when he moved a certain way when his matching white silk jacket opened.

He had rather large hands, but that was obvious from the distance between him and her. When he extended his hand, she noticed that he had a pair of rings on both hands. The diamonds glittered and reflected the sun when he moved his hand at a certain angle. His dress shirt was a bone color but that was dark enough to distinguish itself from his jacket and long silk tie that was also a bleached-white silk.

He was cleaned shaven and wore a big diamond stud in his right ear. Gwen only noticed this when he leaned in, parting his long dark brownish, black pressed, permed hair. But, what was most inviting was his fragrance, which she knew wasn't sold in the bargain department stores.

"*Well, aren't you going to come in for a drink,*" he said, while opening up the door a bit wider.

"No, ... no, I can't. I'm only on my lunch break and they wouldn't like it if I came back with liquor on my breath." Gwen, said while extending her hand for a shake.

"*You mean, you're going to deprive me of the opportunity to show myself as a gentleman? Now, why would you want to make me look bad?*" he said with a smile but now clutching her soft, gentle hand.

"*You still haven't told me your name?*"

Gwen smiled as she felt is warm hand. They were soft like hers. She knew this tall, slender man of maybe 175 pounds with long, straightened black hair didn't get his hands dirty with hard labor. She knew those kinds of handshakes: the dry, callous hands always felt like sandpaper. But, this was soft and long. His fingernails, she also noticed, had a clear polished coat to it. It was better manicured than hers. She made a mental note that if she ever saw him again to find out where he's getting his nails done.

He looked and her and giggled for a second at such a request.

"It's been a long time since someone has asked me what my name is. My name is Jink. And, what is your name pretty lady?" He said with his wide grin.

"Jink! Jink? I've never heard that name before."

She looked up at this face trying to figure if he was putting her on.

"Hi, my name is Gwendolyn Faye, but my friends... some of my friends call me, Gwen."

"Well how do you do, Gwendolyn. That's such a pretty name." He looked intensely in her eyes. "A pretty name for a pretty woman. You know what? I'll call you Gwendolyn because it sounds like the name of a queen." How about that?"

He raised her hand to his lips and kiss the back of her hand.

"My mom and granny gave me that name." Gwen said as she looked down to her feet.

"Well, they sound like extraordinary women to have such faith in naming their daughter such a regal name." Jink said with his arms crossed. "I should know, I know I'm a good judge of character."

"Well... Jenk-" Gwen said but was cut off by the tall stranger. "Jink. Jink, it rhymes with chink. Just think of Chinese food." He said laughing.

"Jink! I think I remember that. Can we do this at another time? I have to grab something and get back to class."

Gwen remembered as she looked at her watch. She recognized that she barely had fifteen minutes left to grab a sandwich and get back to the center.

"What the rush about. Relax. Take the day off."

"I... I can't. I have to get back. Please. Can we talk another time? I have to get lunch, I haven't had anything to eat all day."

Gwen's tone now had a bit of a panic as she realized that she still had a full day of work ahead of her including after school lab work.

"At least, let me buy you lunch? Is that all right? It'll only be about five minutes and you can take it with you."

Jink didn't wait for an answer. He turned to the opened door and snapped his fingers a few times.

"Bobby... Bobby... get me a cheeseburger platter with extra fries and a pickle on the side." He turned to Gwen, "Do you want ketchup and mustard?"

"Yes, please."

"Bobby... Bobby... put some ketchup and some mustard on the burger and put a lot of ketchup on those fries."

He turned from the doorway and looked at Gwen.

"I hope, maybe the next time, I can show you a proper lunch."

"Thank you very much, Jink, but you didn't have to do this." Gwen said, looking in her bag for her purse.

"No, no please. Let me take care of this. I just want to be friends. Let me be a friend." Jink said extending his hand.

Gwen snapped back her purse shut and slowly dropped the purse back in her bag.

"This is so nice of you. Maybe I can buy you lunch next time?"

"I wouldn't think of it. Just your company is all I need."

A tall, statuesque woman came to the door with the bagged lunch. She smiled at Jink but when he handed the lunch over to Gwen, her expression suddenly turned nonchalant. Jink looked at the waitress,

"That'll be all. Don't you have something else to do?"

Gwen was suddenly taken by the exchange.

"I aught to be going now." She adjusted her bag's shoulder strap.

"Well, it was nice meeting you, Jink. Maybe we can have lunch again?"

Jink reached for her free hand.

"I'm sure we will."

Gwen walked off in the direction of the center, not looking back but she heard him say again,

"I'm sure we will."

She smiled a nervous smile.

CHAPTER 18

Before she knew it, Gwen had lunch deliveries over at the center. Cards with funny inscriptions and drivers who had flowers and candies left at the desk. It was a lot for a 16 year old to comprehend, but she was taken by the attention. When she looked at all that Jink was doing for her, she thought about all of the guys she dated in the past and what they didn't do for her.

Several months went by since Gwen and Jink started dating. They became recognizable around Charleston. All of the restaurant-bars knew them. Gwen, the new girl, was now "Jink's woman," and it was a dizzying affair by all accounts: school and Jink.

With all of the things going on, she never knew exactly what Jink did.

When her friends would say, *Where does he work?*, Gwen would always say she didn't know but he had a lot of "business meetings". When she asked Jink what kind of car he drove, he simply smiled and said he was a working man who had friends who'd pick him up and take him to where his work was.

Gwen began to think to herself 'Who are these women who'd pull him aside when they'd walk hand in hand on the sidewalk? Why are they interrupting us when we're eating lunch? Aren't they cold wearing such short dresses?' Jink always had a simple answer, so Gwen just left it alone.

Gwen and Jink planned to have an anniversary dinner to mark their sixth month together. Early on the morning of the anniversary, Gwen received a knock on the door. It was a gentleman who had a rather large box in front of him.

"Jink sent me to tell you that he's looking forward to seeing you this evening! You have a good day, now!"

And, with that he gave her the box, turned around and walked away. Gwen walked in with the package to the surprise of her roommate.

"What in the world is Jink doing?" Gwen asked her friend.

"Girl, I don't know. Does he have a brother?" The roommate asked.

Gwen looked at her puzzled.

"You know, I don't really know. I don't know if he has any siblings. He's never mentioned it to me." Gwen shrugged her shoulders.

"Anyway, if he has any, I'm sure I'll meet them when the time comes.... oh, my Lord.... look at this!"

Gwen pulled out a designer leather bag with the tags still on it. She couldn't pronounce the Italian name but the tiny inscription said, Made in Italy.

"Look at this!"

She held the bag up in the air twirling it around. Her friend reached for the bag.

"Gwen, let me see... oh, my..." The words left her as she looked at Gwen. *"I saw this exact same bag the other day in the window. Do you know how much this cost?"*

Gwen was now looking at a white fur hat and a matching white fur coat. When she pulled the coat out of the box, the coat length went down just below her hips. She walked over to the mirror holding the coat. Without saying a word, she turned to her friend who was still admiring the bag.

"I guess, I'm a long way from Kansas."

Several hours had passed since Gwen returned from the beauty shop. She was beside herself with excitement. She was already fantasizing about Jink proposing to her. How would she tell her mom? Will Michael give her away? It was all too soon. Should she finish school? This feeling was unlike anything she had ever experienced.

Gwen got to the restaurant and there was Jink in a new suit and shoes. He also had his hat tipped to the side. He stood up as she approached and helped her to her seat. Then he leaned over and kissed her on the cheek.

Gwen looked at him and gushed,

"Boy, Jink, you sure know how to treat a girl. Boy, I tell ya, when I tell ya, when I tell ya!"

"Gwendolyn, you're my baby girl. You're my sunshine and my sunflower. You're why the ocean comes in and the bird fly in the air."

A waiter comes over. Jink looks at him,

"I'll have the usual and for the lady... the lady'll have a glass of red wine... the finest you have in stock."

"Yes, Jink. I'll be right back. Here are the menus, let me know when you're ready and I'll take your order." With that, the waiter left.

Gwen didn't want to wait to be served so she worked her way around the table to sit next to Jink.

"I'm so happy!" She squealed.

Jink was surprised to see Gwen jumping up and down in her seat. He knew he found the keys to her heart. He was just about to say something when someone walked up to them in the booth.

"Excuse me, Jink."

A muscular guy with an afro and four inch platform shoes said, as his presence surprised Jink and Gwen.

"Yeah, what is it?" Jink said with a bit of frustration.

"Jink, can I have a word with you for a second." The guy asked politely.

"Can't it wait? Can't you see I'm about to have dinner?"

"Jink, I think it's about that thing we discussed the other day." The guy said.

Jink stared at him for a second then looked at Gwen. Gwen was holding on to Jink's arm, when Jink softly took her hand off of his arm.

"Baby, I'll be right back. I have some business to discuss. I'll be right over here."

Gwen looked but then looked back at the menu dismissing it as some late business matter. She poured over the menu, sometimes struggling to decide what she wanted. 'What do you drink with this? Am I in the mood for that? What is Jink eating? Maybe we can mix and match?'

Just as she finished that thought. Jink came rushing back to the table.

"Gwen. Something's come up. I've got to make this run, I'll be back in less than an hour."

"Where are you going, Jink?" A nervous Gwen said.

"Gwendolyn, I promise I'll be right back. Some emergency's come up at the place where I'm doing business and I gotta' handle it. It won't take long."

Jink leaned in and kissed Gwen, whose look told him that she was disappointed.

"I promise, I'll be right back."

Jink reached into his pocket and motioned for the waiter to come over. As the waiter was on his way, Jink pulled out a cigarette and took a big puff while he tightened his necktie. He snapped his finger and another waiter came bearing his mink coat. Jink pulled out a wad of cash and withdrew a few bills and gave it to the waiter who now was carrying the two glasses they ordered. He peeled off another couple of bills and handed it to the guy who brought his overcoat. Balancing the cigarette in his mouth, he looked to the first waiter and exhaled,

"Give her anything she wants and if that's not enough I'll cover it when I get back."

Jink looks to Gwen,

"Babe, I'll be back in a few minutes, I promise."

The hour hand made it way over several numbers before Gwen found herself nodding at the booth. A waiter came over and asked was there anything else that she'd want because they were closing soon. Gwen suddenly realized that more than five hours had passed and Jink wasn't back.

She was both disappointed and anxious. This was not like him. Where was he? Why didn't he send word about a delay? It didn't matter now. It was late and she had to get back.

***

A week had gone by since that night and Jink was nowhere to be found. Even the people with whom she seen Jink talk to, claimed they didn't know what happened to Jink. She knew they did but why weren't they telling her?

Gwen decided to call the police and file a missing persons' report. After identifying herself as Jink's girlfriend, a voice came back to the line and revealed to Gwen, Jink's real name, his family situation and where he was.

The next morning, Gwen arrived at the holding station and asked to see Jink, referring to herself as his sister. When she saw him in his cell, his neatly pressed hair was unraveled and he now had a full mustache and beard.

"What happened to you, Jink? Why? Please tell me why? Why did you do this? Why did you lie to me? Why didn't you tell me that you're married? Why, Jink? Why? And, what's this about you robbing a warehouse?"

"Hold on baby, hold on. First of all, I'm not really married. That was just an arrangement that she and I worked out. But, she doesn't mean anything to me. I spend all my time with you. You know that. About the robbery, the guy who owns that place owed me money, plain and simple. He owed me a lot of money and I just went there to collect what was mine. Do I look like someone who'd go and rob a warehouse? Do I look like a man who scales walls and climbs through narrow windows?"

Jink said as he held on to the cast iron metal bars.

"But, Jink... what's going on here? I don't understand. What are you doing here? What kind of work do you do for someone to owe you a lot of money?" Gwen said with a heavy heart.

"I'm a business man. I do a little of everything. I invest in businesses. I invest in people. I have people who pay me for my business advice. You could call me a business consultant. A business consultant." Jink said with authority.

It was all too much for Gwen; she thought to herself that she'd have to reorganize his words later. The pressing matter was how were they going to get Jink out.

Jink sat down on the small mattress.

"Baby, I got a court hearing tomorrow morning and the state has offered me a plea deal which I'm strongly considering.

"Plea deal. What does that mean?"

Gwen was more confused than ever.

"It means that they're giving me a choice of either spending some serious time behind bars or I could be out in the community serving as an army recruit. If I take my chance and not take the plea deal, I'm looking at ten in the pen. If I enlist, then all I gotta' do is go over to Vietnam for a couple of years and they'll throw out all the charges."

"You mean, you'll be gone for at least two years?" Gwen said with her eyes starting to bloat.

"It's gonna' be alright. I'm going do my time and when I get out, you and I are gonna' get married. I may be able to talk them into going to Germany, cause I'm may be able to help the police with a different kind of matter that they've been needing help with."

All of this didn't make much sense to Gwen. All she could do was to say,

"I love you and I'll wait for you when you get back."

"Gwendolyn, don't you get soft on me know. I'm coming right back. Two years ain't a long time. I'll be back before you know it."

It wasn't the same, at least not for Gwen. It took her awhile for her to get back into her life as she remembered it before Jink. But the walks down the block and past the restaurants where she and Jink would hang out only reminded her of Jink even more.

She tried reading more and even remembered the real reason for joining the job corps and that was to eventually become a singer. It was these thoughts that she used to replace the images of Jink when her heart would be reminded of the small things he'd do for her.

It was lonely even with her friends around her, but she still looked out of her apartment window hoping to see Jink standing there smiling and waving to her as she opened the shades in the morning.

CHAPTER

Gwen cried many, many nights since she waited at the Grey Hound Bus Station to see Jink off for his trip to Germany. She promised to wait for him however long it took. He told her that he'd becoming back for her.

During those long months afterwards, she stayed inside her apartment she had gotten after she graduated from Job Corps and got a job with the army recruiting office. She'd spend most evenings finding solace in music. One time, she joked to one of her friends that she should just make her own demo and send it off to the record companies. One of her friend's joked,

"Girl, I believe you would be crazy enough to do something like that."

It wasn't long before that comment resonated with her and she began recording herself on cassette tapes and sending them to Motown's LA offices. When she hadn't heard back she started mailing copies to the artists themselves like The Jacksons, Aretha Franklin and Patti LaBelle.

She sang quietly to herself, she sang out loud in the living room and anyplace around her where there was a receptive audience. Time after time, she was told that she has a beautiful voice and that she needed to pursue that calling.

One day, Gwen was visiting downtown Charleston and she went for a walk in the city. She found herself in front of The Juke Box bar. It was in front of The Juke Box that she saw people showcasing their singing talents and it was also the place where she first met Jink. She wondered to herself, why hadn't she returned to the "The Juke" to sing in front of a crowd just to see their reaction. It was now almost a year and she was back in that same spot but without Jink in the picture. But the idea seemed refreshing. Thoughts began to wander around in her head. What if I can go in there and wow the crowd? What if the reaction leads me to a record deal and a singing career? Or what if I bomb? Suddenly the fear of failure didn't feel so threatening as the excitement of trying began to win that battle.

She went in.

There were people there as usual and many people tried their hand with varying results and a few alcoholics who needed the space for their speeches. But for a few brief moments, there was no one in the stage area. Gwen had been sitting down drinking coke when the urge rose up in her to take a chance.

Gwen went to the stage area where a band was performing. The cost of admission was $2 but to perform with the band if you were a singer or an instrument player was priceless. This was Gwen's chance to move past the thoughts of fear that paralyzed her from all the activities that she always wished to do. This was her moment and this was her night to see how far she could go.

For the next three and a half minutes, there was complete silence in the restaurant while Gwen sang. When she finished, she received a standing ovation.

A man came up to Gwen after her performance and extended his hand and introduced himself to her.

"Hello, I am Siese, do you know you've got talent?".
"I do? All I know is that I like to sing, but thank you."
"I mean it. You have what it takes to make it big. What you did up there was incredible. It's been a long time since I've heard something this great from an amateur."
"Thank you, sir. I just graduated from the Job Corps but I really wanna' sing. That's what I feel in my heart to do."
"You can do that. You absolutely can. You've got the talent. Here..." reaching into his pocket, *"this is my business card. Keep it. When you're ready and if you want to pursue a career, I want to help you. I'd love to be your manager. By the way, do you sing any other kinds of music."*

Gwen thought for a second

"I used to sing Gospel... does that count?"
"Sure it does, it's just a different market."
"But, it's been a long time."
"It doesn't matter to me. What's important is that you have a clear

understand of the basics. Knowing the basic means that you're versatile enough to take on any kind of project. But, one thing even more important... take care of your voice. You're going to need it. Take care of it and it'll take care of you."

The gentleman turned around and went back to serving the customers in his restaurant.

For Gwen, this day was one of the happiest she's had in a long, long time. Finally, she thought, someone recognizes my talent and someone is willing to help me get started.

She went home and called one of her friends to see what she was doing. They decided to go out after the friend convinced her that she was sulking far too long over Jink. It was about time she got out. Gwen said she was feeling good and it felt like a good idea.

***

The evening came and they went out to a club not too far from Spiro's. In fact, all night, large groups of people went from one club to another so it was no surprise that everyone was running into everyone all night. However, during the last club she was at, Gwen found herself alone. It was getting late, almost 2 a.m. and the club announced its hours over the p.a. Gwen was getting tired and she had danced the night away. For some reason, in the midst of all the partying, she lost her friend who she came with. Gwen found herself alone, with no friend and no date.

The crowd started to disappear as it got later by the minute. Gwen found herself, by herself. Everything was closing and no one was around. She started to think about how she would get back home. There wasn't a phone around that she could use to call her friend either. There wasn't even a taxicab in sight. She couldn't believe she lost track of time like this. She hadn't had this much fun since Jink left.

With no other option but to walk, Gwen took one step off the sidewalk when she heard someone whistle at her from behind.

"Mmm, Mmm, Mmm! Lookey here, Lookey here! Mmm, Mmm, Mmm!"

Robert Lee said to his friend, Wally Smith, who stood next to him with his arms crossed and nodding.

"My, My, My! Mmm, Mmm, Mmm!"

Robert Lee decided to have a look from the front but by not lifting his head high enough, he failed to notice her raised eyebrow. He smiled as he followed the rainbow on yellow print design of her tunic that went from the gape of the neck and plunged down the V-neckline. The tunic itself flared over a navy blue, beltless, pull-on style polyester pants that flared over her strapped sandals.

She didn't move, now looking straight ahead as if she were the only person on the street. Robert Lee walked around the other side, this time following the slight pulling of fabric over her plump posterior. Wally stood there, still nodding in silent agreement.

Robert Lee had now completed his circle around her.

"*My, My, My! Lady, you sure do know how to make a grown man happy!*"

"Thank you, I appreciate it," she said with a smile.

"*No, thank you!*" Robert Lee said. "*You made my night. As a matter of fact, you made my whole day! What's your name pretty lady?*"

"My name is Gwendolyn, but some of my friends call me 'Gwen' for short."

Gwen said, trying not to show she was perplexed by their unwanted attention.

"Well, Gwendolyn, where are you from? I don't think I've ever seen you before. You sure don't sound like you're from West Virginia."

"No, I'm not from around here. I came because I just got accepted into the job corps. I'm originally from Madisonville, Kentucky."

Wally leaned in while trying to get a glimpse of her cleavage,

"So, where's your man tonight? A pretty woman like you shouldn't be without some protection."

"I feel safe," Gwen said as she turned from Wally to Robert Lee. My boyfriend, Jink, just went to Germany, but he'll be back soon. I'll be alright, 'cause I feel like I know everyone in this town. I even know your family."

"My family?" said Robert Lee.

"Yes, aren't you kin to the twins and you have a sister who works down the street to the left and your mother goes to First Baptist?"

Gwen said with a bit of satisfaction that she had achieved some verbal advantage.

"Your brothers are good guys."

"Yeah..." Robert Lee said as he cocked his head back in surprise.

"Yeah, I got twin brothers, they aaiiight I guess and that what you said about my sister and mother is right. But, let's not talk about them. I don't wanna' waste your valuable time talking about them. I want to talk to you and find out some truths about life and all that good stuff. Maybe, we can we give you a ride somewhere?"

Robert Lee said to Gwen. He then immediately turned to Wally,

"*Wally, get the car.*"

Wally looked surprised by such a request but when Gwen turned her head to see what Wally was about to say, Robert gave him a quick nod and a wink without Gwen ever seeing that communication. He walked away as if going to fetch the car.

Robert Lee turned his attention to Gwen again.

"Where you stay at, Gwendolyn?"

Gwendolyn was hesitant to say, but she blurted out,

"I live out west."

"It would be my pleasure to drop you home or any place you need to go to tonight."

"I don't know, I waiting to see if some friends of mine show up." Gwen said, "They live nearby where I live so we can go home together."

Within 15 minutes, Wally returned with a baby blue 1969 Cadillac Fleetwood Eldorado. Robert Lee walked over and walked to the passenger's side and held the door open,

"I haven't seen your friends and it's getting real late. Why don't you let us give you a ride home Gwendolyn?"

"I don't know. Just let me catch my breath"

Gwen said as she tried to determine the next step to take, but there was also no other option to get back out west. The first bus leaving that area was just after 7 a.m. and her watch read 2:15 a.m.

"Suit yourself," Robert Lee said, *"but I hate to see you not get a ride home tonight, especially being a woman standing here all by*

herself. Come on, let's give you a ride."

Gwen looked at Robert Lee while he was saying it and would occasionally look at Wally who sitting in the driver's seat was grinning from ear-to-ear. She couldn't read their intention but they were right, she would be stranded in the city all night with no where left to go.

"Okay," Gwen said as she slid into the backseat "but I hope I'm not taking you out of your way"

"Don't worry," Wally said, *"you ain't."*

Gwen sat quietly in the back as Robert Lee and Wally mostly talked the typical, vulgar, guy conversations. They'd occasionally ask her if she was alright and needed anything. Sometimes they'd ask if she wanted to go here or there. Each time she responded, it was a simple no thank you, I'm tired and just wanted to go home. It was now nearing 3 a.m. and Gwen's bladder was full.

"How long do you think it'll take before we get to my house?"

Robert looked at his watch,

"I don't know, fifteen, twenty minutes may be even a half hour. Why?"

"I have to pee so bad. Can we stop off some place?" Gwen said holding her side.

Robert Lee looked at Wally,

"Let's take her to my house, it's just right up the street."

Wally smiled,

"Yeah, let's take Jink's girl to your place. By the way, Gwendolyn," Wally asked, "What you see in a cat like Jink anyway. You don't need *some two-bit sucker like Jink. You can have one of us if you'd like."*

Gwen, still feeling like she going to urinate in the backseat, ignored the question by tapping the seat in front of her where Robert Lee was.

"Robert Lee are we there yet?"
"We're almost there, don't you worry about a thing!"

The car pulled up in front of a house. The house was old and dilapidated with broken windows and rotted wood frames. The wooden floor had slabs missing and you could easily see through to the ground below.

"Right over here, young lady! Right over here, you can handle your business and we'll be right here waiting on you to take you home," Robert said as he opened the door to the bathroom.

The bathroom was as filthy as the rest of the house. As she looked more intently as she walked in, she stepped over old dirty soiled clothes and fragments of paper wrappings, and dirty tissue. There was decaying food near the toilet seat, which could have contributed to the wretched smell that aggravated her senses. Scanning the space, she noticed there wasn't any soap anywhere to be seen, much less toilet paper. How does he clean up, she thought as she noticed a shadow cast just beneath the doorway. She could see someone trying to peak through the opening.

"Are you okay in there, Gwendolyn?"
"Yeah, I got a lot to get out of me. It's gonna" take some time" Gwen said.

She urinated as fast as possible as she fought this sinking feeling of fear that started to paralyze her. She mustered enough energy to ignore the fear. When their voices got lower, Gwen very slowly lifted herself off the commode and quietly tiptoed to the edge of the door, hoping that the sound of her getting up wouldn't draw their attention. She leaned into the crack of the door when she heard Robert whispering to Wally. Picking up only a few words clearly, she heard Robert tell Wally

"Let's just get that bitch! Let's tie her up and take her outback. We can have it set up before she comes out.

She was instantly paralyzed; her fear began to grip her as she knew they were talking about her. Shutting her eyes for a few moments, she tried to think of what to do. The only thing she came up with was to run. Gwen waited until there was an opportune time to make her escape, but she didn't know exactly how.

Suddenly she heard the back door open and footsteps walking down the hallway towards a backroom. There was a lot of rumbling and things falling on the floor. She peeked back through the crack and didn't see anyone in her small view. So she opened the bathroom door and closed it softly, leaving the light on. She crept to the front door and again opened it and closed it softly. When she saw that she had made it safely out of the house, she jumped off the porch and saw two directions.

She looked down the dark paved street. A street could get her to something familiar and safe. But a paved road, she thought, would make an easy target if they decided to jump in the car. The second option was the dark woods, which lie between two broken down abandoned houses. This path led to the unknown. She didn't know the area and certainly didn't know where or what lived in the darkness. But with no time to ponder, she had to make a decision and one fast. She started to hear rumblings and shouting in the house, Gwen knew she had to make a move and it had to be made now. She ran straight into the darkness of a field directly in front of Robert Lee's house.

She had gone about 400 to 500 feet before she heard the sound of the men running out of the house calling her name. As she ran deeper and deeper into the woods, she could hear things rustling around her, the sounds of wild dogs and boars in the vicinity were familiar to her. The voices screaming out her name were getting louder and closer. She knew she had to keep running as fast as she could now as the men begin to scream threats on her life, Jink and now her family.

Gwen knew the only way to stay alive was to not look back but to continue to look forward. If she was going to die she thought it was going to be them catching her and not her giving up.

Neither this 3:30 a.m. darkness nor the thickness of these dark hidden trees in her pathway was going to stop her because the voices behind her weren't going to stop either. She had to outlast them she thought, she has to out run them even if it takes all night.

Gwen continued to run unabated every few feet pushing her arms in front of her to detect some kind of intrusion. And what she was able to do with her hands she couldn't with her feet. A part of a root had grown above ground, perhaps through the course of time, had arched upward leaving a space between it and the dirt floor exposed. Gwen's foot got caught in the wedge. The force of her running at full speed and her foot getting caught propelled her more than 10 feet away and over an embankment. She fell flat into a bed of cold, wet leaves that was in a ravine.

It took her a moment to recover and regain a sense of awareness when she realized that Robert Lee and Wally were less than 50 yards away. With her hands and feet, she created an opening in the soggy, decaying leaves and dug her way beneath the surface. She lay there quietly holding her breath.

No more than two minutes later, Robert Lee and Wally were standing over her. She could tell by what they were saying to each other that they were looking for her down the field and perhaps a turn behind them but neither thought to look directly below them. They stood there, she suspected, for about fifteen minutes cursing and plotting what they'd do to her when they caught her.

Gwen laid still underneath the pile of rubble directly below their feet with only her nose sticking out. She laid there silent and awake for the next five hours. She couldn't tell nor could she be certain that they weren't laying-in-wait for her just above the mound. She made a decision that she wouldn't move even if it meant living in the woods for days.

Time had passed, but Gwen couldn't see her watch without rustling up some dirt, but an itch on her nose was beyond temptation. When she scratched her nose, there was light trickling in a kaleidoscope of angles all around her. She begun to slowly part the leaves away from her until the full strength of the sun poured over her face. It was then that she heard a voice above her.

"You're lucky to be alive. I heard the whole thing"

Gwen tried to cover the light from blinding her just in case she needed to run.

"Who is this?"

"I'm sorry, good morning. My name is Mrs. Robinson."

Slowly the image of a short, elderly white woman whom Gwen would have guessed to be in her 70's was standing at the top of the embankment looking down at her.

"Where am I," Gwen asked.

"Oh, dear. You're in back of my house. Would you like to come inside to clean up and may be have something to drink. You're an awful mess, young lady."

Gwen looked at her hands and touched her face. She was happy to be in one piece. But her clothes were torn and dingy from her escape.

"Yes, ma'am. If it's not too much trouble."

"Oh, for goodness sake. It's no bother." The cheerful woman responded.

As Gwen climbed up the embankment and saw Mrs. Robinson, Mrs. Robinson smiled and said,

"Oh, yes. You're lucky to be alive, young lady. You're lucky indeed!"

ACKNOWLEDGEMENTS

A very special acknowledgment to my girls, my daughters in my heart- Stephanie J, Addy, Cynthia, Judy, Ashley B, Stephanie H, Erica, and Britnie. Thank you for loving me in spite of and constantly checking to make sure I was resting.

I want to express my deepest gratitude to several people who have inspired me and kept me motivated when I wanted to quit.

Pastor Bonne' Moon – Thank you for being there whenever I needed you, and your willingness to help in anyway. Thank you for making me laugh. Your door has always been Open to Me.

Shemetris Vital-- You have been the inspiration that has you at every major change in my life. You have a way of just popping up and I get it done.

Michael Lowery, my oldest brother- Thank you for the wealth of knowledge you shared.

Phillip, Phyllis, Thomas and Sharon, my brothers and sisters- thank you for believing in me.

Special thanks to Juliette Ross, for her insight and belief in destiny.

Finally, I want to thank God for giving me the strength to push through. And all of you who patiently waited and believed in me...

THE BEST IS YET TO COME.

CPSIA information can be obtained
at www.ICGtesting.com
Printed in the USA
FSOW01n1906121115
13313FS